Making Mathematics Meaningful

For Children Ages 4 to 7

Werner W. Liedtke

Jennifer S. Thom

Order this book online at www.trafford.com/08-0959
or email orders@trafford.com

Most Trafford titles are also available at major online book retailers.

Co-authored by Jennifer S. Thom.
Cover Design and Designed by Karen H. Henderson

Note for Librarians: A cataloguing record for this book is available from Library
and Archives Canada at www.collectionscanada.ca/amicus/index-e.html

Printed in Victoria, BC, Canada.

ISBN: 978-1-4251-8418-6

*We at Trafford believe that it is the responsibility of us all, as both individuals
and corporations, to make choices that are environmentally and socially sound.
You, in turn, are supporting this responsible conduct each time you purchase a
Trafford book, or make use of our publishing services. To find out how you are
helping, please visit www.trafford.com/responsiblepublishing.html*

*Our mission is to efficiently provide the world's finest, most comprehensive
book publishing service, enabling every author to experience success.
To find out how to publish your book, your way, and have it available
worldwide, visit us online at www.trafford.com/10510*

www.trafford.com

North America & international
toll-free: 1 888 232 4444 (USA & Canada)
phone: 250 383 6864 ♦ fax: 250 383 6804
email: info@trafford.com

The United Kingdom & Europe
phone: +44 (0)1865 487 395 ♦ local rate: 0845 230 9601
facsimile: +44 (0)1865 481 507 ♦ email: info.uk@trafford.com

10 9 8 7 6 5 4

Table of Contents

Dedication and Acknowledgements - 4

Chapter 1 — The Framework - 5
Reasons for the Content - Focus Questions - 5
Aspects of Mathematics Learning - Main Assumptions - 6
Content and Parts - 8
Parents, Preschool and the Early Elementary Grades - 9
Mathematical Language -10

Chapter 2 — Developing Readiness for Number and Counting
Classifying - 11
Specific Goals for Classifying- 11
Open-ended Questions and Tasks -12
Key Ideas and Questions — Selective Activities -13
Young Children and Classifying - Questions and Accommodating Responses - 18
Record Sheet Suggestions -20
Matching - 21
Specific Goals for Matching - 22
Key Ideas and Questions — Selective Activities - 23
About Asking Questions - 27
Record Sheet Suggestions - 30
Ordering - 31
Specific Goals for Ordering - 31
Key Ideas and Questions — Selective Activities - 32
Various Attributes and Contexts for Ordering Tasks - 36
Record Sheet Suggestions - 37
Thinking about Patterns - 38
Specific Goals for Thinking about Patterns - 38
Key Ideas and Questions — Selective Activities - 39
Problem Types for Repeating and Growing Patterns - 42
Patterns and Children's Thinking — Selective Comments - 44
Record Sheet Suggestions - 45

Chapter 3 — Developing Number Sense - 46
Cardinal Number, Numerals and Number Sense - 46
Specific Goals for Cardinal Number, Numerals and Number Sense - 48
Key Ideas and Questions — Selective Activities - 49
Cardinal Number and Numerals to Five - 49
Cardinal Number and Numerals to Ten - 53
Record Sheet Suggestions - 60
Rational Counting - 61
Specific Goals for Rational Counting - 61
Key Ideas and Questions — Selective Activities - 62
Accommodating Questions with Multiple Solutions - 62
Printing Numerals or Number Names - 70
Ordinal Numerals - 71
Specific Goals for Ordinal Numerals- 71
Key Ideas and Questions — Selective Activities - 72
Record Sheet Suggestions - 75

Numbers for Two-digit Numerals - 76
    Specific Goals for Numbers for Two-digit Numerals - 76
    Key Ideas and Questions – Selective Activities - 77
    Ten to Nineteen - 77
    Numbers for Two-digit Numerals Greater than Nineteen - 81
    Record Sheet Suggestions - 86

Operations - 87
    Specific Goals for Introducing Addition and Subtraction - 88
    Key Ideas and Questions – Selective Activities - 89
    Understanding Addition - 89
    Understanding Subtraction - 92
    Further Tasks – Understanding Subtraction - 95
    Record Sheet Suggestions – Understanding Addition - 96
    Record Sheet Suggestions – Understanding Subtraction - 97

Basic Facts - 98
    General Goals for Basic Facts - 98

Equality – Key Ideas and Questions - 98

Basic Addition Facts - 100
    Specific Goals for Basic Addition Facts - 100
    Key Ideas and Questions – Selective Activities - 101
    Practice and Confidence - 110
    Record Sheet Suggestions - 111

Basic Subtraction Facts - 112
    Specific Goals for Basic Subtraction Facts - 112
    Key Ideas and Questions – Selective Activities - 113
    Record Sheet Suggestions - 115

Chapter 4 – Spatial Sense and Measurement Sense
    Spatial Sense - 116
    Three-Dimensional Figures - 116
        Specific Goals for Three-Dimensional Figures - 117
        Key Ideas and Questions – Selective Activities - 118
    Two-Dimensional Figures - 127
        Specific Goals for Two-Dimensional Figures - 127
        Key Ideas and Questions – Selective Activities - 128
    Measurement Sense - 131
        Specific Goals for Measurement Sense - 132
        Key Ideas and Questions – Selective Activities - 133
        Length - 134
        Area - 135
        Capacity - 137
        Weight (Mass) - 138
        Time - 140
        Record Sheet Suggestions - 141

Chapter 5 – Problem Solving and Games - 143

Problem Solving - 143

General Goals for Problem Solving - 143
Selective Strategies for Teaching *via* Problem Solving - 145
Sorting and Classifying - 146
Ordering - 148
Thinking about Patterns - 149
Numbers and Number Names - 150
    Different Names for Numbers - 150
    Different Ways to Show Numbers - 151
    Patterns with Number Names - 153
    Writing Hints About a Number or a Number Name - 153
Operations – Creating Problems - 154
Mental Mathematics Strategies - 155
Spatial Sense - 156
Measurement Sense - 158

Games and Game Settings

Playing Games Their Way - 159
    Commercial Game Settings - 159
    Inventing Games - 162
Games for Number and Number Names - 164
    What is a Game? - 164
    What is a Good Game? - 164
    Lucky – To and From Ten - 165
    Lucky Guess and Lucky Guesses - 167
    Lucky Cover-Up - 169
Suggestions for Record Sheet Information - 170

Dedication and Acknowledgements

For Clara, Dylan, Elliot, Nolan and Samantha.

We hope the ideas in this book will be of benefit to many young children and that the activities, questions and suggestions for conversations will assist children as they begin their journey of trying to make sense of numbers, counting and other important aspects of the early stages of mathematics learning.

We wish to thank our advisors L. Doyal Nelson and Susan Pirie who encouraged us to work with young children, the many teachers who allowed us into their classrooms, and especially the many young children who very confidently participated in activities that involved aspects of mathematical thinking and were always willing to *talk mathematics.*

*A special thank you to Dorothy and Lucas
for their support and encouragement.*

Reasons for the Content – Focus Questions

Impetus: The impetus for this book came from years of working with parents, preschool, pre-service, and elementary schoolteachers. What we have observed as a common theme from these groups was the need for a book of practical ideas that developed and extended young children's mathematics and *mathematical thinking*.

This book is intended for those who are interested in developing and extending key aspects of *numeracy: number sense, spatial sense, measurement sense and sense of relationships* in children ages four to seven.

Goal: We want to share questioning techniques, suggestions for talking about mathematics, methods for accommodating expected as well as unexpected responses, organizational strategies and types of activities for key ideas that we have used with children for developing important aspects of *numeracy*. This sharing of practical ideas is done with a minimum of theoretical discussion. The activities are designed so that they are easy to set up.

A wide range of readily available materials can be used, so there should not be a need to purchase special learning aids. A quick glance at the suggestions for possible materials will give an idea of the types of materials appropriate for the activities that are included in the book.

Content: The content of this book came from actual conversations with children, from questions raised during conversations with teachers and caregivers and from our reflections about these interactions. The following key questions provide the focus for the settings and activities in this book.

What are possible strategies for:

- enabling young children to be successful learners of mathematics?
- assisting and preparing young children to learn and understand mathematics?
- provoking and advancing flexible thinking?
- developing number sense, spatial sense and measurement sense?
- developing visualization skills?
- encouraging, maintaining, and developing a high level of confidence?
- enabling young children to take risks in their learning of mathematics?
- successful problem solving?
- encouraging and developing curiosity and imagination?

Aspects of Mathematics Learning – Main Assumptions

Mathematical Thinking:

> We agree with those who state that there are similarities between *mathematical thinking* and everyday kinds of thinking. One of these similarities is that everything should make sense. This sense making and the development of *mathematical thinking* in general, can be fostered through well-phrased and well-placed questions.

Mathematical Understanding:

> The key indicators of *mathematical understanding* include the ability to talk about what is being learned and what has been learned in one's own words, and being able to connect what is being learned to previous learning as well as to everyday experiences. We believe that well-phrased and well-placed questions can provide opportunities for children to talk about what is being done and to think about their thinking. Appropriate wait time for responses and resisting the temptation to explain can contribute to the development of mathematical understanding.

Problem Solving:

> We believe that children's ability to solve problems is developed in settings where this ability is fostered *via* or *through* problem solving and not by telling them *how to* think or *how to* solve problems. In such a setting, the questions posed require children to suggest possible solution procedures or strategies based on what they know at that particular time in their learning of mathematics.

Number Sense: We believe that *number sense* is essential for successful mathematics learning. *Sense of number* enables children to: make estimates about number; develop *mental mathematics strategies* for the basic facts; develop *personal strategies* for calculation procedures; make *predictions* about answers; and *assess* the *reasonableness* of answers for calculations.

Without *number sense* mathematics learning becomes rote and meaningless. Special settings, questions and strategies are required to foster the *visualization skills* and the *flexible thinking* about numbers that are critical for the development of *number sense*.

Spatial Sense: We believe that *spatial sense*, which includes *measurement sense*, is not only an important component of ability to *solve problems*, but is part of other important areas of learning. Well-phrased and well-placed questions can contribute to the development of *visualization skills* that are necessary for *spatial sense*.

Favourable Characteristics of Mathematics Learning:

We believe that the strategies for the presentations, types of questioning, and suggestions for accommodating possible responses by children that are suggested in the book can foster a high level of *confidence; risk-taking; perseverance; curiosity;* and *imagination.*

Specific Goals and Specific Language:

We believe that *specific goals* are needed not only to provide a focus for activities and settings, but to make assessment possible that is non-subjective and results in reports that are free of general language, or 'edu-speak'. A conscious attempt was made to avoid language that may be difficult to interpret, that is open to misinterpretations, or may even be impossible to interpret. We tried to use language that is mathematically correct.

Children and Mathematics Learning:

We conceive children's mathematics to be an emergent event. The mathematics children learn is a result of engaging in settings that involve physical, verbal, and mental activity as individuals and as members of a group. Mathematical learning is a process of continuous growth. *Mathematical thinking* and *understanding* involve more than a connection of linear ideas and skills. Learning is related to what a child already knows and what a child is coming to know through mathematical and everyday experiences. *Mathematical understanding* is dynamic and ever changing. Since that is the case, any assumptions or conclusions about children's levels of understanding of mathematics at any time are not easily made

Organization of Topics:

Our assumptions about mathematics and *mathematical understanding* shape the answers to the focus questions posed and these assumptions impact the organization of content in this book. Since the learning of many mathematical ideas and skills is not necessarily dependent on how old a child is, but more so on the child's actual mathematical experiences and understandings, a categorizing of activities by age was consciously avoided. Instead, an *open-ended approach* is used and suggested which children four through seven years old can find mathematically inviting and challenging.

The presentation of activity settings for ideas and skills moves from less to more complex forms of thinking. The activities are intended to provide aspects of mathematics and *mathematical thinking* as prompts for children to wonder about, to question their current thinking in relation to the idea or ideas they have of these aspects, and to try and get them to think more deeply about these ideas.

Mathematical activity is not an isolated event; it takes place *in* and *in relation to* the everyday lives of children. Despite a specific focus on young children's learning of mathematics, many *basic thinking strategies* found in the book are not exclusive to the domain of mathematics. As some of the activities will indicate, these *thinking strategies* connect with other important areas of learning as well. We believe that learning about mathematics contributes to fostering the development of language, reading readiness, and evaluative skills that are part of other subject areas.

Content and Parts:

- *Specific learning goals* are identified for each of the topics found in chapters two to four.
- *General learning goals* are identified for problem solving and for the playing of games in chapter five.
- Each topic includes suggestions for activities that deal with important ideas and skills related to the topic. Questioning strategies and suggestions for conversations are included. Ideas for collecting assessment data are outlined on suggestions for entries of Record Sheets. Some of the ideas on these sheets will help a parent and a teacher keep track of the activities that were completed and the comments made during these activities. This form of ongoing documentation provides a starting point for future activities. The comments can be used to create a collection of 'snapshots' of the child's *mathematical understanding*.

Chapter 2: In order to establish a fertile ground from which children's development of *numeracy* can thrive, the essential aspects of it need to be addressed. Since *number sense* is at the core of *numeracy,* it is critical that readiness tasks promote the growth of children's making *sense of number*. In this chapter *basic thinking strategies* necessary for a *conceptual understanding* of *number* and for *rational counting*, as opposed to rote counting, are identified. These *thinking strategies* are not just important for the *understanding of number* and *counting*, but are essential for other areas of mathematics learning as well.

Chapter 3: A wide variety of strategies and possible settings which encourage the development of *number sense* in children are explored. *Rational counting,* the introduction of the *operations,* and teaching about the *basic facts* are discussed.

Chapter 4: The development of *spatial sense*, which includes *measurement sense*, is dealt with as being important for children to be able to interpret their environment in contexts that require *problem solving*. Activities that are favourable for fostering the development of *visualization skills* are presented.

Chapter 5: Since this book focuses on engaging young children to *think mathematically* and on fostering their ability to *solve problems*, the types of questions that are posed are implicit in how children make meaning of their mathematics. The *types of questions* are intended to structure children's *mathematical thinking*; but these types of questions are not limited to a specific context or task, they can be applied to a variety of other settings.

The *key strategies* for *posing questions* that are part of the previous chapters are revisited and discussed in more detail in this chapter. Our reason for this is to communicate and to reiterate that the kinds of questions that are asked, the ways tasks are structured, and how we converse with children directly shape how they may understand the mathematics at hand, as well as their confidence and willingness to take risks. Special consideration is necessary for planning these types of questions and activities so that the potential to promote children's mathematical growth can be maximized. These considerations are discussed and illustrated within the context of problem solving and games.

Parents, Preschool and the Early Elementary Grades

We are what we do: If the old adage, *actions speak louder than words* is accurate then how we interact with children teaches them a lot about what we believe to be true. This does not exclude mathematics, children's learning of it, or their attitudes towards it. Through our interactions with children, we contribute to their learning in many and often unconscious ways such as whether they: remain curious about the world; develop flexible ways of thinking; become effective problem solvers; love to learn; or take risks in their learning. With this in mind, the goal is to develop ways of interacting mathematically with children that promote and nurture these attributes and abilities. These types of interactions with children can encourage their enjoyment; their confidence and an *'I-want-to-understand'* attitude; and invite them to think creatively so that they may take their *imaginations* beyond what is here and now, and wonder, *'what if…?'*

Nothing in the world is ever as simple and straightforward as we might first assume it to be. Often, taking a closer look, reveals everything to be surprisingly complex. The same can be said about mathematics and mathematical activity. Let us try to communicate to children that there is always more than one way to think about a given problem and often, more than one way to solve it. One way that we can communicate to children that we consider *their mathematics* and *mathematical thinking* to be complex, is to avoid closing off potential opportunities for them to learn by labeling their responses simply as, *right* or *wrong*. Whether a response appears to be identical, close to what we anticipate it to be, or completely different than what we expected, by accepting what a child says or does can open a space for us to move deeper into understanding the thinking that gave rise to the response, a possible space for further exploration. More often than not, the reasoning connected to a child's responses possesses valid and even logical aspects of *mathematical understanding* and *thinking*.

Mathematical Language

The ability to recite mathematical terms and phrases without understanding their meanings is not an indicator of *mathematical thinking* or of *mathematical understanding*. Although we agree that the acquisition of appropriate and correct language is necessary, in many contexts, it is not the aim when learning about something new. Whenever possible, discussions with children about mathematical ideas and practices should first begin with natural or everyday language. In most instances, it will take time for children to learn and use the actual mathematical terminology.

When we do choose to use mathematical language in our conversations with children, we need to be mindful to use terms in an appropriate and correct manner. This requires caution when using terms that have more than one meaning. This includes words commonly found in everyday conversation. A list of examples includes: *number* and *amount*; *number* and *number name* (numeral); *pattern* and *design*; *guess* and *estimate*; *figure* and *shape*; as well as assigning names of two-dimensional figures to three-dimensional figures – for example, calling a *cube* a *square*.

It is also beneficial that those who are working with young children use correct and consistent meanings for mathematical terms. For example, the meanings for the following terms *basic fact*; *game*; *problem solving*; *triangle*; *rectangle*; and *circle* could differ among participants while taking part in a discussion, or even for authors who write about mathematics teaching and learning. Children should also learn to use the correct language when comparisons are made that involve numbers or amounts.

Fostering the development of *mathematical thinking* and *mathematical understanding* is a challenging journey, a journey that can be interesting as well as enjoyable for everyone involved – children, their parents and the teacher.

Classifying

Classifying involves an important *mental strategy* not just for mathematical ideas, but for other areas of learning as well. In general, it consists of observing a common attribute of certain members in a collection and grouping those objects that share the common attribute.

With young children, common attributes for classifying are colour, shape and size. One reason for engaging children in classification activities is to develop flexible thinking about properties that go into making up classes of things. This flexibility makes it easier for children to move from categorizing classes based on direct perception to using other criteria for classification such as *numerousness* or *number properties*.

The ability to consider *numerousness* as an attribute across classes is necessary for making sense of more formal work with number. In this chapter classifying is discussed as a separate topic. However, the pervasiveness of this strategy will become obvious as it resurfaces in other parts of the book with respect to different aspects of learning mathematics.

Specific Goals for Classifying:

Children will be able to:
- identify and explain attributes other than colour, shape and size as means for classification.
- demonstrate *flexibility* in their thinking by classifying objects and groups of objects in at least two or more different ways and explain the methods for classification.
- use *numerousness* as a way to classify groups of objects.

In addition to these specific goals, the related focus questions and the main assumptions made with respect to *mathematical thinking*, *mathematical understanding* and *problem solving* provide the guidelines for the activities, the strategies and the questions that are suggested in this chapter.

(continued next page ...)

Classifying (cont'd)

Open-ended Questions and Tasks

Open-ended tasks and *open-ended* questions are necessary for addressing the general goals, the specific goals, as well as encouraging children's *confidence*, *risk taking* and *flexibility in thinking*. For clarity, the example illustrates the difference between a *closed* or *heavy-handed* task with one that is *open*. Two completely different manners are requested while considering the same mathematical context.

A child is facing articles or drawings of food and clothing. To ensure that all objects can be recognized, the child is asked to name each member of the collection. The request is made, *Put all those that you can eat in one bunch and all those that you can wear in another bunch.*

The task as posed does little, if anything, to encourage a child's thinking because the thinking has already been determined. Not only that, the manner in which the child is to think about this activity is so specific that it *disables* any opportunity for the child to develop any different meaning for the task. The *closed* nature of this activity makes it simply a task of following the instructions, or just busy work. It does not engender any sense of wonder or questioning on the part of the child.

In contrast, the task becomes radically different when the child is asked to examine the members of the collection and is requested to, *Pick out the items that you think are in some way the same. Explain how you think they are the same.*

Rather than telling the child *what* and *how* to think, this task as posed, enables all sorts of possibilities in terms of how it might be conceived and ways of responding to it.

The inclusion of, '...*you think* ...', with an emphasis on '*you*', in a question or request encourages *risk taking*. *Confidence* is also fostered, since the young child learns to realize that the response to this type of question or request will not be classified as right or wrong.

Any indicators of risk taking should be praised. This acknowledgement can lead to further risk taking and build confidence which, in turn, leads to more risk taking.

Let's Find Another One

Possible Materials:

A collection of:

- stamps,
- leaves,
- rocks,
- or buttons.

Very young children can be introduced to sorting by asking them to select and isolate one object from a collection and then requesting,

- *Try to find another object that you think is in some way the same as the one in front of you.*
- *How do you think these two objects are the same?*

Once this type of task has been repeated and several objects have been selected, children can be asked to try to,

- *Explain how you think all of the objects are in some way the same.*

Once three or four objects have been selected and deemed to be the same in some way, pose the question,

- *Which of these do you think is in some way different?*

This request can get children to examine similarities and differences in more detail as well as having children discover similarities not considered before.

Birds of a Feather

Possible Materials:

Pictures or drawings
of similar animals
like birds
or fish.

The child is asked to look at the collection and select a few that are in some way the same. **Flexible thinking** is encouraged by repeating this task. After a similarity has been explained, the animals are returned to the collection. Then the request is made,

- *Try to think of another way of picking out animals that are the same in some way.*

Depending on the child's response, this procedure could be repeated several times.

Questioning:
During this activity, it may be tempting to ask questions in the form,

- *Is there another way of ...?*

This may be interpreted by children as a *closed* question prompting a response of, *'No'*. Then there was the child who responded to this type of question with, *'Yes, what else?'*

Instead, responses are more likely to be forthcoming if the requests begin with,

- *Try to ...;*
- *Show me how you would ...;*
- *Explain what you think ...;*
- *What do you think ....*

Here They Come Again!

This activity is similar to the previous Let's Find Another One

Possible Materials:

Collections
of toy animals.

Several animals are sorted into two groups and placed onto two pieces of paper. Each group has a common attribute that the child tries to guess. The child is asked,

- *How do you think the animals on each piece of paper (or in each pen) are in some way the same?*

The procedure is repeated several times, but each time the collection of animals is sorted according to a different characteristic. For example:

- tall – short
- long tail – short tail
- tame – wild
- big ears – small ears

Each time the request is made,

- *Here they come again!*
- *How do you think they are in some way the same?*

At times hints can prompt the discovery of new similarities.

After several rounds of this activity, switch roles and challenge the child to try and think of still different ways of sorting the same group of animals.

Flexible thinking can also be fostered in a larger group setting by asking children to demonstrate to others how they have not only classified a group of objects, but classified it in many different ways.

Reactions like, *'Oh yeah'*; *'Neat'*; and, *'I never thought of that'* serve as indicators that new ways of thinking about a collection have been discovered.

Could Not Belong

Possible Materials:

Sets of four similar but not identical objects or pictures.

For example:

• toy animals such as horses or sheep;

• pictures of animals or flowers.

As the child faces a set of four, the following question is posed,
- *Which of these do you think is different?* <u>or</u>
- *Which of these do you think does not belong?*

Flexible thinking is encouraged by asking,
- *Which other one do you think could be different?*

Some children may become so *flexible* in their *thinking* that they identify each member of a set to be different in some way.

This could be a goal for these kind of settings.

Each time a child selects a member and identifies it to be different, a similarity for the other members of a set is identified, even if it is not verbalized.

To encourage *flexible thinking*, a member could be selected from a set and the child is asked to try and guess the reason(s) why the person selected it.

This task can be carried out by looking at four pictures of people or children, or by looking at children themselves, with the proviso that we do not say anything about anybody that they would not like or that might be hurtful.

A Definite Difference

Possible Materials:

Four different blocks or drawings of blocks.

For example:

• square-based pyramid;
• sphere;
• cone;
• cylinder.

As for the previous task, a setting where the child is asked,
- *Which of these do you think is not like the others?* <u>or</u>
- *Which of these do you think is not the same?*
invites the child to consider more closely, similarities and differences.

After selecting the object which is in some way different from the others, the child is asked to explain the reason(s) for choosing that particular block.

To encourage *flexible thinking*, the selected block is returned back to the group of blocks and the child is asked,
- *Which other block do you think is in some way different?*
- *How do you think it is different?*

Some children may benefit from a few hints that are given. These could include,
- *Try to think about something that the blocks remind you of?*
- *Where in your house or your yard have you seen something that looks like these blocks?*

A Likely Characteristic

Possible Materials:

Drawings of
alien creatures
that are
colourful – some
of the same colour.

The major goal for the tasks that involve classifying deals with trying
to foster *flexible thinking* and to get the child to think of characteristics
other than colour, shape and size.

Sometimes it may be advantageous to remind children that colour
can be used but try to think of something other than colour. At some
point it is a good idea to use objects that are relatively similar in size,
different shapes, and are either colourless or the same colour.
Colour could be used as a possible distractor, as is the case for this
example.

As the child looks at the group of creatures the request is made,
- *Try to find some creatures that you think are in some
  way the same.*

After a selection is made, the child is asked to describe what the
creatures have in common. The child is then challenged to try
and find other common characteristics,
- *Is there anything else that is the same about them?*

Returning the creatures back with the rest of them and inviting the
child to find still other ways in which two or more creatures are in some
way the same encourages the child to search for different solutions.

**Accommodating
Responses**

It may be necessary to keep reminding the child to think of something
other than colour or size.

One Difference or More

Possible Materials:

Sketches of several nametags on graph paper where each letter of a name is printed in one square:

- Nolan
- Clara
- Mike
- Maria
- Corinne
- Caren
- Christine
- Samantha
- Dylan
- Eliot

The child faces a collection of nametags, e.g., of friends, family, members of a play group. After being told that the tags are names of people, the challenge of trying to find something that might be the same for some of the names is presented.

Asking a child to identify and describe the differences can lead to the discovery of new similarities.

It is not necessary for the child to know how to read in order to participate in this activity. It is possible for the child to identify qualities such as:
- *long,*
- *short,*
- *looks the same at the beginning (or end),*
- *has a curly thing here, etc.*

What Could It Be?

Possible Materials:

- Pieces of paper with different numbers of chips or buttons.

- Three pieces which show the same number, i.e., four buttons.

- Paper plates or pieces of paper with objects that are as different as possible, but two or three of the plates have the same number of objects, i.e., three objects.

As a child, in turn, faces each of the settings, the question is,
- *Do you think there is anything that is the same for these pieces of paper (or plates)?*

Depending on the response (or responses) the following question could be asked one or more times,
- *Try to find something else. Is there anything else that is the same?*

This setting is not intended to be a test, but it does provide an opportunity to find out whether a child recognizes and uses **numerousness** as a classification strategy.

Young Children and Classifying

**Questioning
and
Accommodating
Responses**

When young children face a box of 'stuff' or a 'junk' box made up of pieces from different toys, many times they will select items that are in some way the same even if they have not been asked to do so. Usually the strategies used to select pieces are obvious, since these are likely to involve colour, shape or size.

However, there are times when the responses to,
- *Try to pick out some things that you think are in some
  way the same*
are not obvious and we must ask the child.

For instance, how could anyone possibly guess these two children's methods of categorizing things,
- *'These are interesting, and these are not.'*
- *'These are yummy, and these are yucky.'*

The activities in this section are examples of how everyday materials and contexts can be used to create inquiries that involve genuine questions and curious problem solving settings about classification. In addition to these, children might also identify similarities and differences amongst such collections as: art; seashells; stories; poems; plants; summer activities; songs; favourite books – the list goes on.

Classification activities can become part of everyday experiences as similarities and differences are discussed. Magnets or photos on the fridge are an example of an ideal setting that is suitable for a simple ***Guessing Activity***. Whenever faced with different types of objects or pictures of objects, it is easy to select a few and to pose the challenge:
- *Guess how I think these are in some way the same.*

**Accommodating
Responses**

Guesses are not classified as right or wrong. Credit is given for what a child was thinking of as each guess was made. If, by chance, the goal is to aim for a specific response, hints are provided until the guess is correct. Then the child can be given a turn to select and to respond to guesses.

A similar activity that has differences as the focus can involve the selection of three or four objects or pictures, pointing to one of these and having the child guess why it might be identified as being different. A response to the request implies that similarities for the remaining members of the set have been identified. Repeating the request encourages ***flexible thinking***.

Children in a group can simulate this setting by looking at three or four members of the group and thus discover many similarities and differences about themselves and the things they wear.

(continued next page ...)

Young Children and Classifying (cont'd)

The major goal of the classification activities is to foster **flexible thinking**. An indicator of *flexible thinking* would be if a child looks at several members of a collection, for example: **[S] [T] [7] [L]** each printed on different pieces of paper, and explains how not just one but how two, three or ultimately each member could *'not belong'* and describes how the particular object is different in some way from the rest.

Accommodating Responses

Responses like, *'One has a roof'* or, *'This one has curves'* are possible responses to an *open-ended* question like, *Which one do you think is different?* whereas in *closed* settings only one response is accepted as correct. If the goal is for a child to identify the number name as being different and a child keeps talking about the other members of the set, the question and the instructions need to be made specific. Here a hint like, *Think about letters of the alphabet*, is necessary .

Record Sheet Suggestions

Keeping a record of some of the sample responses that were part of the activities and problem solving settings related to *sorting* and classifying provide a snapshot of what children did at a given time. Adding responses to these records as tasks and problems are revisited or presented in different environments provide indicators of growth with respect to the goal of sorting, classifying and **flexible thinking**. The suggestions listed below serve as a guide to prepare a record sheet for a child.

Since **open-ended** questions and problems involve the accommodation of all types of responses they can contribute to fostering **confidence** and **risk taking**. Indicators of these favourable characteristics of mathematics learning should be noted and kept track of.

1. Strategies used for **Let's Find Another One**. _____

_____

2. Indicators of flexibility – list of objects that were *classified* in more than one way and the strategy used for sorting. _____

_____

3. Responses to **A Definite Difference** and reasons for selection. _____

_____

4. Responses to **A Definite Difference** that identified more than one difference. _____

_____

5. Attributes successfully identified while playing **Here They Come Again!** _____

_____

6. Differences identified and described for **Could Not Belong.** _____

_____

7. Differences and similarities identified for **One Difference or More.** _____

_____

8. Response to task for *numerousness* as a *sorting* strategy – **What Could It Be?** _____

_____

9. Indicators of *confidence* and *willingness to take risks*. _____

_____

Matching

If young children are to learn how to *classify* according to **numerousness** or **number**, they need some way of determining when the number of objects in different sets is the same and when it is not. They need to be able to sort the groups of objects that share the same number into one class and to *not* include those groups in which the number of items is different.

Many children have learned how to recite the names for numbers at an early age. While reciting these names, they may skip some, stop whenever they feel like it, or recite them in orders of their own liking or ability of recall. Children may reach a point when they correctly match number names with objects; determine that there are six little cars and six big cars, but will conclude for the latter, *'This six is more.'*

In most cases, young children who are counting are doing so in a mechanical sort of way. Although the process of counting with understanding entails *matching* or *one-to-one correspondence,* it is only one of several *mental strategies* that children need to consider before they count with understanding or *count rationally*. At an early stage when learning about *numerousness, rational counting* is too contrived for young children. For now, the attention is focused on engaging children to respond to prompts such as,
- *Are there just as many?* <u>or</u>,
- *Are there the same number of ...?*

It is important to note that neither of these questions asks,
- *How many in each?* <u>or</u>,
- *How many are there?*

Children learn that *matching* or *one-to-one correspondence* is used to find the solutions to two types of problems:

After a group of counters is presented, one of the following requests is made,
- *Without any counting, try to find as many objects.*
- *Without any counting, try to find the same number of objects as there are in this group* (the group pointed to) *of objects.*

After several groups of counters, some with the same number of counters, are presented, the child is requested to,
- *Without counting, try to find out which groups contain the same number <u>or</u> just as many objects, and which groups do not.*

This activity requires children to physically move and rearrange objects. If a match is made, then
- *there are the same number of ... <u>or</u>,*
- *there are just as many of 'one' as of the 'other'*

can be used as part of the description of the outcome.

(continued next page ...)

Matching (cont'd)

If a match cannot be made, the groups do not have the same number of items. In this case, the labels,

- *not the same number*;
- *not as many*;
- *more;* and
- *fewer*

can be used as the outcomes of the *matching* are described.

The label *fewer* is used when discrete objects in groups are compared, rather than the term *less*.

The term *less* is used for comparisons involving continuous quantity <u>or</u> *amount,* like capacity.

Once learned, *matching* or *one-to-one correspondence* is a simple strategy for young children to use. Look for opportunities in their everyday activities, i.e., setting the table, playing with blocks or toy animals, to use *matching* and have a conversation about the results.

Specific Goals for Matching

Children will be able to:

- establish two equivalent sets *without* counting.

- demonstrate and explain how two sets are equivalent regardless of different appearances with respect to shape, size and/or colour.

- demonstrate and explain that rearranging the members of one of two equivalent sets does not change the equivalence.

- establish three or more equivalent sets and describe the relation between the number of objects in the different groups as possessing *the same number,* or each group possesses *as many* objects.

- describe the relation between the number of objects in sets that do not *match* by using such words as: *more, fewer, not as many* and *not the same number of....*

As the following activities are presented, remind children to try to do these without counting.

They're the Same

Possible Materials:

Sets of
finger arrangements,
or drawings of sets,
are used as master sets.

Hold four fingers up and ask the child to,
- *Hold up just as many and show the same number of fingers.*
- *Without counting, how can you show that you are holding up as many or the same number of fingers?*

The number of fingers held up is varied and the same requests are repeated.

After a set of fingers is shown, challenge the child to respond to,
- *Use a different arrangement of fingers to show just as many or the same number of fingers.*
- *What is the same for the groups of fingers?*
- *What is different about the groups of fingers?*

For some children the reminder that thumbs are considered to be fingers may be required.

Make Them the Same

Possible Materials:

A row of six objects
that are the same
size and shape,
such as:

- bottle caps,
- buttons,
- or other objects,

and
more than six
of the same objects
in another group.

Present the row of six objects and request,
- *Look at these* (the objects in the row are pointed to) *and without counting try to pick out just as many.*
- *How do you know you have picked out as many?*

The aim is to have children use their own words to describe *one-to-one correspondence.* Sample comments might include:
- *'I picked one out for each one of these.'*
- *'There is one for each one of these.'*
- *'Each one of these has one of those.'*
- *'I matched each one of them.'*

If children insist on counting, acknowledge the response but then repeat the challenge,
- *How is it possible to tell without counting?*
- *Try to show that there are as many buttons in each group without counting.*

Same and Different

Possible Materials:

Two rows of seven
or more
identical objects such as:

- buttons,
- bottle caps, or
- pieces of macaroni.

Present the two rows of counters and pose the task,
- *Without taking any counters away and without putting down any more counters, try to make one of the rows of counters look different.*

After the task is completed, the child is asked,
- *What is different about this* (the row is pointed to) *and this* (the new arrangement is pointed to)?

To find out whether a child recognizes that number has not changed as a result of rearranging the objects, ask the following question,
- *What is the same about the row and what you have made?*

**Accommodating
Responses**

It must be kept in mind that the descriptions of similarities could include references to such things as the type of materials the objects are made of; or the shape, size, or colour of these objects. Since that is the case, the request to compare the two arrangements may have to be repeated several times.

Little Spoons – Big Spoons

Possible Materials:

- Six or more small spoons (or forks) in a row.

- Ten big spoons (or forks) in a bunch.

The row of spoons is presented. The child is reminded not to count and the following requests are made,
- *Try and pick out as many big spoons as there are little spoons in the row and show that there are just as many.*
- *How do you know there are just as many little spoons as there are big spoons?*

The small spoons or the big spoons are picked up and held tightly in one hand.
- *How do you think the two bunches of spoons are different?*
- *What do you think is the same about the two bunches of spoons?*

**Accommodating
Responses**

The responses will indicate whether a child understands the idea that no matter what is done to the objects, as long as no objects are added or subtracted, the equivalence between the two groups is preserved.

This idea may take some time to develop. Telling a child what the answer should be is not likely to short-cut the required time to develop this understanding.

Different Shapes

Possible Materials:

- Cut-outs of seven small triangular shapes placed in a row.

- Cut-outs of ten big square-shaped shapes in a bunch.

The purpose and the questions are the same as for *Little Spoons – Big Spoons* where *size* was the identifying attribute. In this setting the defining attributes are *shape* and *size*.

The following request is made,
- *Without counting, try to pick out just as many square-shaped pieces as there are in the row in front of you.*

For a comparison of the two groups, pose the following questions,
- *What do you think is different about the two bunches of shapes?*
- *What do you think is the same about the two bunches of shapes?*

The child who has stated, *there are the same number'* or *'there are just as many of each'* can be faced with the scenario of seeing all of the selected shapes placed in a stack.
- *What can you tell or say about the number for each bunch of shapes?*

Just as Many

Possible Materials:

- Cut-outs of nine happy faces arranged in a circular shape.

- Cut-outs of twelve sad faces in a bunch.

Accommodating Responses

Variations:
The task could be presented several times by arranging the objects in a different way.
<u>For example</u>: in a triangular shape; in a square shape; as an oblong; or in a figure eight. The number of objects to be matched could be increased.

The child is faced with the requests,
- *Without counting, try to find as many sad faces as there are happy faces.*
- *Explain and try to show why there are the same number of each.*

The small spoons or the big spoons are picked up and held tightly in one hand.
- *How do you think the two bunches of spoons are different?*
- *What do you think is the same about the two bunches of spoons?*

For some young children keeping track of the starting point, the spaces between the faces, and the end point can present a challenge. If that is the case, redirection might be in order by again asking the child to try and think of a different way of showing that there are the same number for each type of face.

If, as part of the solution strategy, the child rearranges the row of the happy faces, make the following request,
- *That is one way of doing it. Try to think of another way of finding as many sad faces without rearranging the happy faces. Explain your thinking.*

Set the Table

Possible Materials:

- Six plates.

- Ten spoons.

- Ten eggcups or saucers.

Since the focus for these activities is on matching, the reminder to *try to do this without counting* should always be kept in mind.

Six plates are on a table and the child is asked to help set the table.
- *Pick out as many spoons as there are plates.*
- *How do you know there are as many spoons as there are plates?*
- *Find as many eggcups (or saucers) as there are plates.*

After the table is set, the child is asked,
- *What do you think is the same about the spoons and the eggcups?*

If *'just as many'* or *'the same number'* is part of the response, the child is asked to explain the reason for this response.
- *What do you think is the same about the plates, spoons and eggcups?*

Several experiences of this kind may be all that is required for a child to make comparisons for three sets.

Extension:

If the child is able to generate appropriate conclusions about *one-to-one correspondence* across three sets, a fourth set could be introduced. For example, an egg for each eggcup, or a cookie (block) for each saucer.

The focus of the observations should be on what the child explains or demonstrates in terms of the *number* of:
- eggs (cookies),
- eggcups (saucers),
- plates; and the number of spoons.

Once the results of *matching* or *one-to-one correspondence* are understood, they can be transferred to any number of counters and the correct conclusions will not be influenced by distractors, even in cases when these are somewhat extreme.

The next two activities and the corresponding questions are designed to determine whether or not a child's responses are influenced by distractors.

Copy Me

Possible Materials:

- Two clear glasses of the same size.

- A collection of beads or counters of the same size.

The child is requested to drop a bead into a glass every time an adult or another child drops a bead into another glass. The intent is not to count as the beads are dropped into the glasses. One attempt to discourage counting can include the carrying on of a conversation of some type while the beads are dropped into the glasses.

After about fifteen or twenty beads have been dropped into each of the two glasses, ask the child,

- *Do you think there are more beads in your glass, more beads in the other glass, or are there the same number of beads in both glasses?*

Regardless of the response, follow the question with,

- *Why did you say that?* or, *How do you know?*

If the child answers correctly and reference to *matching* is made in some way, the beads from one glass can then be poured onto the table or onto a plate and the child is asked,

- *Do you think there are there more beads in the glass, more beads on the table or are there the same number of beads on the table as there are in the glass?*
- *How do you know?*

About Asking Questions:

The question prior to the, *How do you know?* is rather lengthy, but there are valid reasons for this being the case.

First, when asking a child to compare the number of beads, the three choices need to be presented. Often, children are only given two options,

- *Are there more beads in this glass or more beads in the other glass?*

This may lead children to assume that there are more beads in one of the glasses and consequently, respond incorrectly.

Second, as the task resumes and more beads are dropped into each jar, asking a question such as, *Are they still the same?* can and does prompt some children to respond with, *'No.'*

Given this, an adult might come to the conclusion that such a response indicates a lack of understanding of *matching*. However, responding *'No'* could very well refer to the fact that,

- *They are not the same because they look different from before* or,
- *They are different now because we put more beads into the jars.*

These types of questions should end with the characteristic being considered, in this case, *number*.

Copy Me Again

Possible Materials:

- Two clear glasses.

- A collection of small beads or counters and another of large beads or counters.

Accommodating Responses

The questioning and the strategies are the same as for **Copy Me**, but what is different about this activity is that *small* and *large* objects are used; that is, each time a *small* object is dropped into one glass, a *large* object is dropped into the second glass.

As in the previous activity, distractions may be necessary to discourage counting as the objects are dropped. There are some children who insist on counting during the task and still others who will count even after the question has been asked.

Two possible responses that can be encountered are:
- *There are more beads in my glass* or, something like,
- *They are the same number, but my twelve is more.*

Both of these responses provide valuable information about a child's level of understanding of *matching*.

How do we respond when children's conclusions are based on perception? For most young children *seeing is believing*, and that is how it is, and it may remain like that for some time. Putting the correct response into a child's mouth does not shorten this time. Development of understanding takes time. However, we believe that even if the answers are not what we expect them to be, having listened to the questions that are part of these tasks is a learning experience.

The results of *matching* and children's conclusions should be talked about whenever the opportunity arises. It could be that some of the tasks may need to be revisited several times.

Extension for *Copy Me Again*

Possible Materials:

- Two different clear glasses, one tall and skinny, the other shorter and wider.

- Two boxes of beads, one with small round beads, the other with larger beads – different shapes.

Children who have a working knowledge of *one-to-one correspondence* and the appropriate conclusions will not be distracted by extreme perceptual variables, no matter how tempting they may be.

The purpose of **Copy Me Again** is to not only engage children in a setting in which there are such distractions, but to provide them with the opportunity to reflect on and question their previous understanding of the results of *matching* as well as the meanings of *as many* and *the same number*.

The strategies and questions are the same as for **Copy Me**. Each time a small bead is dropped into the short and wide glass, a large bead from the other box is dropped it into the tall and narrow glass.

Show and Find

Possible Materials:

- Three paper plates or pieces of paper with three, four and five counters or buttons, respectively.

Four fingers are held up.
The following questions are made,

- *Hold up just as many fingers.*
- *How can you show that you are holding up as many fingers without counting?*

Then child is requested to,

- *Point to the plate that you think has as many buttons as there are fingers. How do you know?*
- *Show me that there are just as many or the same number of buttons without counting.*
- *Look at your fingers and the other two plates. What can you say and show about the number of counters on these plates?*

The child's responses indicates whether appropriate comparison language is used. Does the child use *'more'*, and *'fewer'*, rather than *'bigger'* and *'smaller'*.

The child may need to be reminded to respond to the questions and the requests without using the names for the numbers *'three'*, *'four'* and *'five'*.

Record Sheet Suggestions

Any responses that are recorded should contain information about the key ideas related to *matching*:
- How does the child establish *equivalent sets* without having to count?
- Is the comparison language that is used to describe objects in groups that match and objects in groups that do not match appropriate?
- How does the child demonstrate that using objects that differ in size; in shape; or in size and shape does not in any way distract from establishing equivalent sets?
- How does the child demonstrate that once equivalence is established, changing the arrangement of the members in one group does not change the equivalence?

1. Strategies demonstrating there are *the same number,* or *as many objects in each group* – ***They're the Same; Make Them the Same.*** _____

    _____

2. Strategies showing there are *not the same number, not as many, fewer,* or *more objects* in one set than another – ***Same and Different.*** _____

    _____

3. Comments and/or reactions when *matching* the objects to be selected were

    - different shapes _____

    - different sizes _____

    – ***Little Spoons – Big Spoons; Different Shapes.***

4. Comments and/or reactions when the arrangement of one matched set was changed – ***Same and Different.*** _____

    _____

5. Language used to describe the members of two sets that are equivalent or match – ***Little Spoons – Big Spoons; Different Shapes.*** _____

    _____

6. Comments and/or conclusions when three or more equivalent sets of objects were considered – ***Set the Table.*** _____

    _____

7. Language used to describe the number of counters in sets that do not *match* – ***Show and Find.*** _____

    _____

8. Reactions to a *matching* example when extreme differences exist – ***Copy Me*** and ***Copy Me Again.*** _____

    _____

9. Indicators of *confidence* and *willingness to take risks.* _____

    _____

Ordering

Ordering plays an important role in the understanding of certain mathematical ideas and is part of other areas of learning as well. When children *sort* and *classify*, they need to find a common characteristic upon which to base their classification. In *ordering* tasks beyond the simplest settings, children must isolate a common attribute and then order the objects in the set according to the magnitude of that attribute. The questions that are posed focus on *order* or on the *relations of order*.

Ordering is not just a requisite of *mathematical thinking*, but it is also necessary for language development and reading. As far as *mathematical thinking* is concerned, we want young children to know what we mean when we *order* or *put objects in order;* how to describe how adjacent objects differ from one another in an ordered sequence and use this to justify the position in the sequence; and how to use a wide variety of characteristics in problem solving settings dealing with order.

Specific Goals for Ordering

Children will be able to:

- copy a set of odd-numbered objects in a linear arrangement and describe how the linear arrangements are the same.
- copy in reverse or backwards a set of odd-numbered objects presented in a linear arrangement and explain how the arrangements differ.
- explain how two adjacent objects in an *ordered sequence* differ by making reference to the appropriate attribute.
- use an *ordered sequence* of objects as a model to construct their own *ordered sequence* for a different attribute and explain how the sequences are the same and how they differ.
- extend an *ordered sequence* in both directions and justify the placement of the objects by making reference to the magnitude of the appropriate attribute.
- insert into an *ordered sequence* members that differ from those in the sequence and members that are the same as a member of the sequence and justify the positioning by making reference to the magnitude of the appropriate attribute.
- after constructing *ordered sequences* in different directions; left to right, right to left, downwards; upwards; diagonally; draw conclusions about ordering and directions.
- identify and select the next member in one of two *ordered sequences* that has been reversed and justify the selection by making reference to the magnitude of the appropriate attribute.
- use pictures to create an ordered sequence and tell a story for the ordered pictures.
- conclude that changing the *order* of the pictures can result in different yet coherent stories.

Neighbourhood Street

Possible Materials:

- Seven different blocks
  – all in a row, i.e.,
  cylinder, sphere,
  square-based pyramid,
  cube, cone,
  half of a sphere,
  rectangular prism.

- A collection of blocks
  that contains at least two
  of each of the blocks
  listed and a couple of extras.

If blocks are not available,
pieces of cardboard
cut into different shapes
can be used.

The simplest idea of order deals with the notion of *being next to.*
Ask the child to,
- *Think of the blocks as houses along a street.*
- *Look at the houses on the street.*
- *Use these other blocks and try to make another street of houses that looks just like this one.*

Once the task is completed, pose the following questions,
- *How are the two streets the same?* or,
  What is the same about the two streets of houses?
- *How do you know your street is exactly or just like the one you looked at?*

Backwards Street

Possible Materials:

- The same as for **Neighbourhood Street**, but the blocks or cardboard cut-outs are placed in a different order.

Seven blocks or cut-outs are placed in a row and the child is told to think of these as houses along a street. The request is made,

- *Choose blocks and try to build another row of houses that is backwards from the one you are looking at.*

For some young children the term *backwards* needs to be illustrated. This can be done by selecting a copy of the first member of the model row of houses and placing it at the opposite end of the model street,

- *If this one belongs here, which one do you think should be next to it if this row of houses is to be backwards?*

If necessary, this could be repeated with a copy of the second house on the original street.

The reason for using an odd number of blocks and for making duplicates of the blocks available now becomes obvious. When the child gets to the middle part of the sequence, the going backwards becomes a special case. Rather than going backwards, it is a direct copy.

If the idea of *being next to* is not understood, the child will continue the row of houses by copying rather than going backwards, because copying is much easier. Without the duplicate blocks, this response is not possible and consequently, the materials would dictate the answer – and the task would be a *closed* one, rather than being *open-ended*.

Accommodating Responses

It is important to consider: What might be done if a child reverts to copying? One course of action is to ask the child to explain or try to explain the problem that was presented at the beginning. Another option might include saying to the child,

- *What do you think about putting this house* (i.e., the appropriate choice) *in this spot?*

These types of intervention may result in some children correcting themselves. Their responses might include such expressions as, *'Oh yeah! I forgot'* and having them carry on building the street of houses in a backwards order instead of copying part of the original row of blocks. However, there are other children who do not realize that a mistake has been made and they will carry on with copying.

Still other children realize that a mistake has been made, but in order to save face, they do not acknowledge the correct response. If errors are not recognized, it is best to leave things as they are and revisit the task again later.

Sticks and Rings

Possible Materials:

• Seven sticks or straws
of different lengths
placed in order – a common
baseline or starting point.

• A collection of plastic rings
of different sizes
or rings of different sizes
made from
pieces of wire.

Invite the child to,
- *Tell something about these sticks.*
- *What do you think was done with these sticks?*

If this *open-ended* approach does not prompt a discussion about the relative length of the sticks, more direct requests are required. For example:
- *Look at these sticks. Point to the longest stick.*
- *Look at these sticks. Point to the shortest stick.*

As two adjacent sticks are pointed to, ask the child,
- *How do you think these two sticks are different?*

Explain to the child that when the sticks are arranged like this, we call it **putting them in order** or **ordering the sticks**. Request the child to,
- *Take these rings and try to put them in order just like the sticks are in order.*

After the task is completed,
- *How do you know they are in order?*
- *How do you know the order you put them in is the same as for the sticks?*
- *How are two rings that are next to each other different?*

Order the Cups

Possible Materials:

• Five cups or glasses
of different sizes
in an ordered sequence.
• Cups or glasses;
one larger and one smaller
than those in the
ordered sequence.
• One cup or glass
that fits into the
ordered sequence.

Accommodating Responses

The ordered sequence of cups is presented,
- *How are two cups that are next to each other different?*

A cup *larger* than those in the sequence is presented and the child is asked,
- *Where do you think this cup belongs?*
- *Why do you think it belongs there?*

Repeat the same two questions, but this time give the child a cup that is *smaller* than those in the sequence and a cup that fits somewhere in the sequence.

If a child uses the words *'bigger'* or *'smaller'* as part of the responses, ask the child to try and think of other ways to describe the difference between adjacent cups.

Just the Same

Possible Materials:

• Five different weights, or five pieces of cardboard of different sizes in an ordered sequence.

• Weights or pieces of cardboard that insert into and extend the ordered sequence in either direction.

• One weight or piece of cardboard that is exactly like one in the ordered sequence.

As for **Order the Cups**, this activity involves the child extending an ordered sequence in both directions and inserting members into the ordered sequence.

However, for this setting ask the child to determine the placement of an object that is *exactly* like one that is already part of the ordered sequence.

After a piece of cardboard that is identical to another piece of cardboard in the ordered sequence is presented ask the child, .
  • *Where do you think this piece of cardboard belongs*?
  • *Why do you think it belongs there?*

For a few children the solution consists of not placing the object into the sequence because, *'they all have to be different.'*

Cookies on Plates

Possible Materials:

• Six paper plates of different sizes or circular cardboard cut-outs in an ordered sequence

• Six square-shaped cardboard 'cookies' of different sizes.

The request is made to,
  • *Place a cookie on the plate where you think it belongs.*

It is predictable that for most of the children the order for the cookies will the same as for the plates, *'small cookies go on small plates and big cookies go on big plates.'*

Take the cookies off the plates. Place the smallest cookie onto the biggest plate, and ask the child,
  • *Which cookie do you think should go onto the next plate?*

Such an invitation may prompt some children to see that it is possible to reverse an ordered sequence, while other children may argue that, *'you cannot do that.'* These children are at a stage when *'big'* things can only go with other *'big'* things and it may take time and many more experiences before this changes.

Various Attributes and Contexts for Ordering Tasks

Engaging children to extend *ordered sequences*, insert members into the sequences, and having children use appropriate language to describe how the magnitude of adjacent members differs can be applied to a variety of attributes and settings.

- several glasses of the same size filled with different amounts of water or juice. What can children say or demonstrate about the sound made as each glass in the ordered sequence is tapped gently with a spoon?

- several sticks of different thicknesses or diameters, but of the same lengths. What descriptors do children use to describe adjacent members in an ordered sequence?

- several pieces of paper identical in size that are of different shades of the same colour. How do children describe the shades of colour in the ordered sequence?

- name tags that have letters recorded on graph paper, one letter per square. How will children describe adjacent names and how will they deal with two names that have the same number of letters?

- several containers of identical shape and size, e.g., small film canisters filled with varying amounts of sand. How do children attempt to solve the problem of ordering these from lightest to heaviest?

- four cartoons, e.g., different stages of a doghouse being built, and four adjacent rectangular regions that the cartoons can be placed into.

  After the children place the picture they think *happened first* and the picture they think *happened last*, the remaining pictures are placed between these. Ask the children to tell a story about the sequence.

  The children are asked whether or not they think another sequence for the pictures is possible. A positive response is followed with the request to tell the story that would go with this sequence.

- four plastic cups or dishes of different sizes in an ordered sequence. Four paper plates or pieces of paper, equal in size, with two, three, four, and five cookies, or drawings of cookies, of the same size on them. The following questions are posed,
  - *Which plate do you think should go with which cup? Explain your thinking.*
  - *What is different about the cookies on the plates that are next to each other?*

Record Sheet Suggestions

The information on record sheets should reveal whether or not a child:
- uses the appropriate language to describe the magnitude of adjacent members in an *ordered sequence.*
- constructs an ordered sequence and explains why it is done correctly.
- extends an ordered sequences in either direction and inserts into the sequence and justifies the moves that are made.
- considers different ways of creating ordered sequences

1. Observations related to the task dealing with *next to*
   – **Neighbourhood Street** and **Backwards Street**. _____
   _____

2. Examples of correct terminology used to describe the magnitude
   of the attributes of adjacent members in an *ordered sequence.* _____
   _____

3. Comments and observations of activities that involved:

   - *extending* an ordered sequence – **Fill the Cups**. _____
     _____

   - *inserting* into an ordered sequence – **Just the Same**. _____
     _____

   - dealing with two objects that are the *same* – **Just the Same**. _____
     _____

   - *constructing* ordered sequences – **Sticks and Rings**. _____
     _____

4. Comments and observations made when one of the
   ordered sequences was *reversed* – **Cookies on Plates**. _____
   _____

5. Observations made for the *ordering* **Cartoons** activity. _____
   _____

6. Indicators of *confidence* and *willingness to take risks.* _____
   _____

Thinking About Patterns

Closely associated with the study of *order* is the examination of *patterns*. In non-mathematical settings, the term *pattern* is sometimes used when *design* would be more appropriate. In mathematics, *pattern* refers to something that is in some way predictable. This means that in mathematics we may make the distinction between designs and *patterns* as well as designs that contain patterns.

Patterns can *repeat*, (a b c a b c ...) or *grow* or increase ([**], [****], [******], ...), and one type can very easily be converted into the other. Various options exist for changing these patterns. For example, for the repeating pattern, two of each letter could come next and then three of each letter, etc., and for the skip-counting by two pattern, the two, four and six counters could be repeated.

Activities that involve *patterns* provide opportunities for children to develop *flexible thinking* and stimulate their *imagination*. It all depends on the types of problems that are presented.

A *closed* question that asks, *What comes next?* without giving any other specific information, which has as its answer key one possible solution, can be detrimental to a child as far as fostering *confidence* and *willingness to take risks* is concerned.

Accommodating Responses

For example, consider the child who responds to the question, *What comes next?* by changing a *repeating pattern* into a *growing pattern* or vice versa; continued a pattern in a unique way; or used the given pattern to generate a new pattern. All of these responses would be labelled as incorrect or wrong, especially on a written test with one answer identified as correct. Such an assessment on a test indicates to a child a lack of understanding patterns. Responses by a child during a follow-up conversation may indicate such a conclusion to be completely incorrect.

Specific Goals for Thinking About Patterns

Children will be able to:
- identify, describe and explain in their own words what a *pattern* is.
- explain how a hidden member in a *repeating pattern* can be identified.
- consider different attributes for building and extending *repeating patterns.*
- explain how a hidden member in a *growing pattern* can be identified.
- explain how and why a *repeating pattern* can be extended in different ways.
- explain and show how a *repeating pattern* can be changed into a *growing pattern.*
- explain and show how a *growing pattern* can be changed into a *repeating pattern.*

Who is Hidden?

Possible Materials:

• Several copies of
pictures or sketches
of boys and girls,
or two types of toy animals.

• A piece of cardboard
for a screen.

The goal of this setting can
be reached by using any two
types of objects, i.e., rocks
and leaves, or spoons and
forks.

The question for this setting
is, **What is Hidden?**

Out of view from the child, the pictures or objects are used to create
a *repeating pattern*. One of the members of the pattern is hidden
behind the piece of cardboard.

The child is engaged with the following types of requests,
- *Look at the pictures of the boys and girls.*
- *If there is a child under the piece of cardboard,
  do you think it is a boy or a girl?*
- *Why do you think so?*
- *Do you think it has to be what you said it is? Why or why not?*

The child is told,
- *When it is possible to tell or predict what is hidden by looking
  at the other things in a sequence, we call that a **pattern**.*
- *If we keep on placing pictures, objects or things in the same
  way, we call that a **repeating pattern**.*
- *If the pattern with the boys and girls is a repeating pattern,
  who would be next and why?*

What is Hidden?

Possible Materials:

• Pattern blocks or pieces
of coloured paper
cut into different shapes.

• A piece of cardboard
for a screen.

The key questions are the same for each of the types of settings.

The purpose is for the child to consider different attributes
as part of the recognition of patterns.

For the examples with the blocks, children are told that they
are looking at a *pattern*.

The following questions can serve to structure the discussions:
- *What do you think is hidden behind the screen?*
- *Why did you say that or how do you know?*
- *What do you think should come next and why?*
- *What would be next and why?*

Thinking About Patterns

Pattern of colour and shape.	Different figures cut from coloured paper or coloured interiors of different shapes: dark square, dark triangle, white circle, dark square, [screen], white circle.
Pattern of shape independent of colour.	Different figures cut from coloured paper or coloured interiors of different shapes: two red triangles, blue rectangle, two green triangles, red rectangle, one yellow triangle, [screen], orange rectangle.
Pattern of colour independent of shape.	A random use of different types of blocks: blue block, yellow or colourless block, blue block, yellow or colourless block, blue block, screen, blue block, yellow or colourless block.
Patterns – variations of the above examples with two members of the pattern hidden behind the screen.	Different figures cut from coloured paper or coloured interiors of different shapes: triangle, two squares, triangle, two squares, [screen], square, triangle, two squares.

Hide and Seek

Possible Materials:

• A collection of two types of objects. For example, paperclips and pencils, or spoons and buttons.

Ask the child to create two different *repeating patterns* using the objects.

With the child's eyes closed, hide one or two members of each of the patterns behind a piece of cardboard.

After the child's eyes are opened ask,
- *What do you think is behind the piece of cardboard?*
- *How do you know? Explain your thinking.*

Have the child lift up the piece of cardboard and check to see whether the response was correct.

More Cookies

Possible Materials:

- Four paper plates
  or
  pieces of paper.

- Small round counters.

Place the plates in a row. In a linear vertical arrangement place two counters or cookies on the first plate, four on the second, and six on the third plate.

Ask the child to look at the plates of cookies and,
- *Show on your fingers how many cookies there are on* (the first plate is pointed to), *the first plate.*

Tell the child,
- *To figure out how many cookies go onto the second plate, a match is made with the cookies on the first plate and then two more cookies are placed onto the plate.*
- *For the next plate, a match is made with the cookies on the last plate and two more cookies are placed onto the plate.*
- *The same procedure of matching and two more is used for the next plate. If this is continued, we have a **pattern** because we can tell or predict what comes next. Since there are more cookies each time, this is called a **growing pattern**.*

The child is requested to,
- *Use the same procedure to put cookies on the next plate.*

Once the task is completed, make the request,
- *Without counting, show me with your fingers how many cookies you think would be placed on the next plate.*
- *Why did you show 'this' many fingers? How did you figure that out?*

Hide one plate behind a piece of paper and ask,
- *How could you figure out how many cookies are hidden?*

Now What?

Possible Materials:

- Figures
  cut from cardboard,
  or toy animals
  are used to show a
  growing pattern.

  For example:
  Triangle – square – circle – two
  triangles – two squares – two
  circles – three triangles.

Make the following requests,
- *Pretend that you are looking at a repeating pattern, what would you put down next and why? Explain how you would continue your pattern.*

- *Pretend that you are looking at a growing pattern, what would you put down next and why? Explain how you would continue your pattern.*

Got Rhythm and Shape

A Rhythmic *Pattern* **is presented.**	For example: Clap – stamp, stamp – clap, clap – stamp, stamp – clap, clap, clap – stamp, stamp.
A Body Movement *Pattern* **is presented.**	For example: Tall shape – short shape – tall shape – short shape – short shape – tall shape – short shape – short shape – short shape.

Problem Types for Repeating and Growing Patterns

a) Recognition of the *Pattern*

After presenting the pattern, ask the child to repeat the pattern. If the response is correct, ask the child,
- *How did you know what to do?*

Accommodating Responses

If the response is incorrect, two possible scenarios exist.

The child may think it was done correctly. If that is the case, the response to the question, *How did you know what to do?* provides valuable insight into what important information may be missing.

If the child knows that the attempt was not correct, a response to, *Why do you think that happened?* Can yield valuable information about a child's understanding.

b) Extending a *Repeating Pattern*

If the child has successfully repeated the *pattern* after hearing it, the suggestion is made,
- *Try to think of a repeating pattern and continue the rhythm* (or *sounds*).

The responses, correct, thought to be correct and incorrect are accommodated as suggested for the previous problem.

c) Extending a *Growing Pattern*

The procedure and the accommodation of possible responses is the same as for **Recognition of the Patterns**, but the request this time is,
- *Try to think of a repeating pattern and continue the rhythm* (or *sounds*).

These three problem types can become part the **Body Movement Pattern** discussions.

How Many? – I Wonder

Possible Materials:

• Four paper plates, or pieces of paper, in a row.

• Objects or counters.

The first plate with one paper clip, or object; the second plate with three paper clips; the third plate with five paper clips, but hidden under a piece of cardboard; and the fourth paper plate with seven paper clips.

The child is faced with the problem,
- *How could you try to figure out how many paper clips there are on the plate hidden behind the piece of cardboard?*
- *Do you think there are any other ways of figuring this out?*
- *Explain how you would continue the pattern.*

An *open-ended* request could be,
- *Do you think there is another answer to the question, What comes next?*

Try Again

In the spirit of expecting the unexpected, this next task is to encourage children to take risks in their mathematics and give them an opportunity to use their imaginations.

Possible Materials:

• Three different objects to display a simple repeating pattern.

For example:
spoon – fork – knife – spoon – fork – knife.

The intent is to have the child respond to,
- *What do you think could come next?*
- *Try to think of as many ways as you can to extend the pattern.*

After each suggestion ask the child to explain how to extend the newly created pattern.

A record is kept of the different responses.

Upon completion, the child can be asked to sort these responses into *repeating* and *growing* patterns.

Patterns and Children's Thinking

Selective Comments

Documentation plays an important role in *advancing* a child's *thinking*.

For example, if a child knows of only one way to extend a given *pattern*, and a sketch or photograph of the response is made and kept, it can be used at a later date to encourage the child to reflect on what was done and to try to go beyond this previous response.

As the drawing or picture is examined, the child is reminded,
- *This is what you did last time, try to think of other possible ways of showing what you think could come next.*

Accommodating Responses

Patterns **are predictable, but children's responses may not be.**

If life unfolds in unpredictable ways, why should we expect anything less of children's mathematical activity?

For the *pattern* of different shapes: **triangle – square – triangle – square – triangle – square,** five year-old Tommy responded to the question, *What comes next?* by selecting a circular shape. When asked why he had done so, he stated, *'I want to see a circle.'*

Taken at face value, it could be concluded that Tommy did not demonstrate an understanding of *repeating patterns*.
Rather than ending the conversation at this stage, Tommy was asked,
- *What would you put next?*

He proceeded to build a *repeating pattern* with the six previous figures that was more complex, and perhaps more interesting to him, than the one he was originally presented with.

Then there was the young boy who knew that the object he selected did not fit the given *repeating pattern*. He justified his selection by stating,
- *'I know what comes next, but I like this one* (pointing to the object) *much better.'*

Such 'logic' should not be debated!

Record Sheet Suggestions

The possibility that exists of extending *patterns* in different ways presents a challenge when attempting to gain insight into a child's understanding of *thinking about patterns.*

Since it is not easy to construct assessment items that require a high degree of specificity, a brief conversation provides the richest and most revealing information about a child's thinking.

1. Words used in definition of *pattern* –
   Who is Hidden? and **What is Hidden?** _____

   _____

2. Strategies used to predict and describe a hidden
   member in a *repeating pattern* – **Hide and Seek**. _____

   _____

3. Strategies used to identify a hidden member
   in a *growing pattern* – **More Cookies**. _____

   _____

4. Explanations used for extending r*epeating patterns*
   – part of **Got Rhythm and Shape**. _____

   _____

5. Indicators of *flexible thinking* – **Try Again**. _____

   _____

6. Indicators of *confidence* and *willingness to take risks.* _____

   _____

Number Sense

The comments and activities in this chapter illustrate how the *mental strategies* of *classifying* and *matching* are requisites for fostering an understanding of *cardinal numbers*. These numbers are introduced in random order because the intent is to show how the *mental strategy* of *ordering* and ideas related to *thinking about patterns* are requisites for *counting rationally*.

The importance of *number sense* as a requisite for learning about the *basic addition* and *basic subtraction facts* is illustrated.

The introductory comments that follow include the answers to the questions:

- What is *cardinal number*?
- What do we mean when we say *number*?
- What is a *numeral*?
- What is *number sense*?

Cardinal Number Numerals and Number Sense

One attribute of any set of discrete objects is *numerousness*. This *numerousness* is labeled *cardinal number* or often referred to simply as *number*. *Cardinal number* or *number* shows *how many*. We use *number names* or *numerals* and *symbols,* such as *four* and *4*, to label an attribute of a group of discrete objects, or the common attribute for all of the groups that have the same answer to *how many*?

The *matching* activities introduced children to the notion that *one-to-one correspondence* can be used to determine whether the relation between the number of objects in a set and the number of objects in other sets is equal or not. We assign the same *number name* or *numeral* to the sets that have the same number of objects, no matter how the characteristics of the objects in these sets differ.

The *classification* activities are intended to make children think flexibly when they think about attributes used to make up classes of things. This flexibility should make it easier for children to move from an understanding of classes based entirely on perceptions such as colour, shape, and size, to developing other criteria, such as *number* or *cardinal number*.

One difficulty young children face is that sets of discrete objects can have something in common even if they do not share a single physical attribute. The *matching* activities show children that sets can belong to the same class when objects in each set can be placed in *one-to-one correspondence* with objects in every other set. Thus, three elephants can belong to the same class as a group of three fleas. For a child who relies heavily on perception such discrepancies may be hard to overcome. It may be difficult for such a child to get rid of the notion that there are *'more'* elephants, *'This three is more'*, and to realize that the property considered, *three* or *threeness*, is independent of colour, shape, size and arrangement.

(continued next page ...)

Number Sense (cont'd)

Children need to learn that when they consider the number or numerousness of sets of objects, they cannot be distracted by the colour, shape and size of the objects. Children need to realize that rearranging the objects in a set does not change the numerousness of that set.

At some stage a child may insist on solving every problem by counting, which may be nothing more than the repeating of nonsense syllables. Some children claim to 'know all the numbers'; and indeed, the way they recite number names can be quite convincing. However, these same children may also assert that, 'The four over here is more than the four over there.'

It is a great achievement for young children when they gather up several different looking groups with the same number of objects, i.e., five; state that there are the same number in each group; name the property, i.e., 'five'; and select a card with the numeral **5** printed on it because they know that symbol describes the class of all sets that have *fiveness* as a common property. This property is labeled *cardinal number*.

The general goal of the activities with *cardinal numbers* and *numerals* is for children to make sense of these numbers. The aim is to foster the development of *number sense*, the roots for *numeracy*, without any reliance on counting and that is the reason for dealing with *cardinal numbers* in random order. Ideas related to *ordering* and work with *growing patterns* are then used to learn how to *count rationally*.

Aspects of *number sense* include:
- *visualizing* numbers.
- *recognizing* numbers without having to count; *subetizing*.
- *flexible thinking* about numbers.
- *estimating* numbers.
- *connecting* numbers to experience.
- *relating* numbers.

(continued next page ...)

Number Sense (cont'd)

**Specific Goals
for
Cardinal Number,
Numerals
and
Number Sense**

Children will be able to:

- recognize and say the *number name* for a small set of objects or for an arrangement of fingers.
- describe how several differently arranged sets of objects showing the same *number* but differ: according to colour; according to shape; according to size; and according to colour, shape and size are the same and how they are different.
- point to or select from several choices the *numeral* that describes a given set of objects or an arrangement of fingers.
- select the appropriate number of objects or show the appropriate number of fingers for a *number name* that is given orally.
- recognize and name, without having to count, a *number* to five that is briefly shown and for *numbers* from six to nine that are shown with similar objects in familiar arrangements.
- show a given *number* in at least two different ways and explain how the displays differ and how they are the same.
- indicate *how many more* are needed to show or to get to five or ten.
- use the *referents* five or ten to *estimate* whether a number that is briefly displayed has *more* or *fewer* objects than the *referent*.
- give examples of where in their experience *numbers* and *number names* are seen and used.
- use terms like *greater than*, *less than*, *close to*, *between*, and *far apart* when numbers are compared or related to one another.

Cardinal Number and Numerals to Five

Finding Fives

Possible Materials:

- A *master set* for the *cardinal number* five – a picture or drawing of five dots in a linear arrangement;
  or a drawing of fingers on one hand;
  or the fingers on a hand.

- Four pieces of paper:
  two with five dots
  or with five similar counters;
  one with three dots
  or three similar counters;
  one with two dots
  or two similar counters.

- A card showing – **5**.

Five is well suited to introduce children to *cardinal number*, if for no other reason than having five fingers on one hand. These fingers are also well suited for a *master set* for the *cardinal number* five, since it is easy to use them for tasks that involve *one-to-one correspondence*. Prior to the task, several pictures or designs that show groups of five could be displayed somewhere. For example, five butterflies, five birds, five letters of the alphabet, etc.

Hold up five fingers and tell the child,
- *Whenever we can match the objects in any group with this many fingers, we call it or name it five and this is the number name for five*, as **5** is pointed to.

The child is requested to,
- *Look at the counters on the pieces of paper and try to find those groups that you think show fives.*
- *Use the fingers on your hand to show that each one is five without counting.*
- *Try to find other fives. How do you know each one shows a five?*
- *Find an example of a bunch or group that does not show a five.*
- *How can you show that it is not five?*
- *What words can you use to tell about the five fingers and the group of counters that is not a five?*

If deemed appropriate, carry out the task by showing the child a card with the number name **five** along with the numeral **5**.

Houses and Rooms

Possible Materials:

- A box of building blocks of the same size.

- Several pieces of paper.

The child is requested to,
- *Find five blocks for each piece of paper.*
- *Show how you can do this without counting.*

Pretend each block is a room of a house. On each piece of paper (i.e., land), use the five rooms and try to build houses that all look different in some way.
- *How are the houses different?*
- *What is the same for all of the houses?*

Further prompts may be required for the child to conclude that the houses look different since the rooms are arranged differently and they may be of a different colour, but they have the same number of rooms, or show the same number – **five**.

Different Looking Fives

Possible Materials:

- Sticks of the same length and shape – toothpicks or popsicle sticks.

- Small scraps of coloured paper of different sizes and shapes.

- Pieces of paper.

- Glue.

The requests are similar as for *Houses and Rooms*.

The child is given four pieces of paper.
- *Use five sticks on each piece of paper and try to make designs that look different.*

The follow-up discussion focuses on what is different about the designs and what is the same. For the sticks, colour, shape and size are the same, but the arrangements differ. The child may suggest that the designs are reminders of different things and for some designs the sticks are close together or far apart, but they all show the same number – **five**.

For the designs created with the pieces of coloured paper, the colours, shapes, sizes as well as the arrangements of the pieces differ, yet the designs all show **five**.

The settings and questions for *Houses and Rooms* and *Different Looking Fives* are modified for introducing the *cardinal numbers* three and four and the respective numerals, **3** and **4**, and if appropriate, the words **three** and **four**.

Match the Name

Possible Materials:

- Pieces of paper or paper plates with dots or counters to show the *cardinal numbers* five, three, four, two, zero, and one.

- Cards with the numerals **0**, **1**, **2**, **3**, **4**, and **5**, in random order and, if appropriate, on separate cards the number names **zero**, **one**, **two**, **three**, **four** and **five**.

In random order, hold a number of fingers up. After each display, ask the child to,
- *Hold up just as many.*
- *Show that just as many are held up without counting.*

Then make the request to,
- *Point to the plate* (or piece of paper) *that shows as many or the same number.*

Tell the child the name for *that many,* as the appropriate numeral (**0**, **1**, **2**, **3**, **4**, **5**) and number name (**zero**, **one**, **two**, **three**, **four**, **five**) are selected and placed beside each appropriate *cardinal number*.

The fact that **zero** is a number name for the cookies on an empty plate needs to be pointed out.

Differences Aside

Possible Materials:

• Four pieces of cardboard or paper, each with five chips or dots that are arranged in different ways.

The chips are the same size, but differ in colour.

Accommodating Responses

Invite the child to,
• *Look at these pieces of paper*, as the four pieces are pointed to.
• *Tell me what you think is different about them?*

Shift the focus to,
• *What do you think is the same about them?*

This question has many possible answers. Children are observant. They may say such things as, *'They all have chips/dots.'*; *'They are all on pieces of paper'*; and, *'These all have a ... (naming a colour) on them.'*

It may take several repetitions of, *What else do you think is the same?* before some children will actually make reference to *cardinal number.* .

Extensions:
Five or six pieces of paper, or paper plates, and objects that differ according to colour, shape and size, i.e., scraps of coloured paper or pattern blocks, are used to show *cardinal number.*

If this setting proves to be too difficult for a young child, then objects of the same size and shape should be used.

Finger Flash

Possible Materials:

• Fingers or drawings of counters on pieces of paper.

For a *Finger Flash* setting, a number of fingers is briefly shown, i.e., four, long enough to be seen, but not long enough to allow counting.

The child is asked,
• *Tell me how many do you think you saw?*

This task provides insight into a child's ability to recognize and name numbers without having to count. This ability is sometimes referred to as *subetizing*.

If drawings of counters are used, they can be drawn on one side of a folded piece of paper or cardboard. This piece of paper is briefly unfolded for a quick glance at a number.

Initially, the counters in these drawings should be the same size and shape. The level of difficulty can be changed by increasing the number of counters or by changing the size and shape of the counters that are drawn.

Show and Change

Possible Materials:

- Fingers or drawings of counters as for *Finger Flash*.

Hold up several fingers, i.e., four. Invite the child to,
- *Hold up just as many or the same number of fingers.*

After the child holds up *as many*, shows that there are *as many* without counting, and names the number, make the request,
- *Show your number in a different way* or,
Make your number look different.

Accommodating Responses

Some children hold their fingers closer together or upside down. These responses meet the condition of the request. Some children may use both of their hands to show the same *cardinal number*, demonstrating *flexibility* in their thinking about number, a very desirable abstraction. Children who do not use both hands, need to be invited to do so. The follow-up questions for each response are, *What is different?* and, *What is the same?*

The question, *What is another different way?* encourages children to go beyond the initial response.

Greater Than and Less Than

Possible Materials:

- Fingers or drawings of counters, as for *Finger Flash*.

When discrete objects in different sets are compared, the descriptors *fewer*, *fewest*, *more* and *most* are used, i.e., there are *fewer* cookies on this plate and *more* cookies on the other plate.

However, when the comparisons involve the *numerousness* or *cardinal number* property of sets, the terms *less than*, *least*, *greater than* and *greatest* are used, i.e., the number of cookies on this plate *is greater than* the number of cookies on the other plate.

Hold three fingers up, or show a group of three counters.
Invite the child, in turn, to use fingers to show:
- *a number that is greater than three. Name the number.*
- *a number that is less than three. Name the number.*
- *a number that is less (greater) than three and close to three. Name the number.*
- *a number far away from three. Name the number.*

Repeat the procedure with different numbers.

Imagine

Possible Materials:

- Fingers or drawings of counters as for **Finger Flash**.

This task contributes to the development of *visualization* skills.

Flash fewer than five fingers and invite the child to,
- *Tell me how many do you think you saw.*

Then make the request,
- *Show me on your fingers how many you think you did not see* or,
- *Show me with your fingers how many more you think it would take to show five fingers.*

It may be necessary to remind the child that a number name for *no fingers* being shown or held up is *zero*.

Cardinal Number

and Numerals to Ten

The main *goal* is to foster *number sense* without relying on or emphasizing counting. That is why *cardinal numbers* are dealt with in random order. The *specific goals* remain the same as for numbers and numerals to five.

One possible sequence of presentation could be: **seven**; **nine**; **six**; **eight**; **ten**.

Rather than repeating the key activities for each *cardinal number*, one of these is dealt with in detail. Similar activities and settings should be used for introducing children to the remaining *cardinal numbers*.

Listen and Feel

Possible Materials:

- A glass jar
  or a small tin can.

- Pennies or small marbles.

A different aspect of *visualization* is encouraged when a child is asked to think about number with eyes closed.

With the child's eyes closed, select and drop several marbles (or pennies) into the jar. Drop them into the jar so that it is difficult or impossible to count the objects.

Before each drop prompt the child to,
- *Think of five fingers. Listen to the sounds as the marbles are dropped into the jar.*
- *Try not to count.*
- *Tell whether you think there were more or fewer than five marbles dropped into the jar.*
- *Explain how you decided on your answer.*

Repeat the task and prompts as numbers from zero to nine are chosen.

A similar setting is created when the child, with eyes closed is asked to,
- *Listen to the number of knocks on the table* (or on a door).
- *Do you think there were more or fewer than five knocks on the table?*
- *Explain how you decided on your answer.*

Unevenly spacing the knocks discourages counting.

As the child sits with eyes closed, fingers are used to repeatedly touch the child's arm or shoulder. The touching is done in a way that makes counting difficult or impossible.
- *Do you think you were touched fewer or more than five times?*
- *Explain how you decided on your answer.*

Create another setting that involves touching by placing small blocks onto a paper plate. Spaces are left between the blocks. However, the spacing is such that a child's open hand can cover all of the blocks. After the child closes the eyes, blocks are placed onto the plate. The child's hand is guided over the plate and downward onto the blocks. As the blocks are touched, the child is asked,
- *Do you think you can feel more than or fewer than five blocks on the plate?*
- *Explain how you decided on your answer.*

About Seven

Possible Materials:

- Seven fingers or a sketch of seven fingers.

- Pieces of paper showing the word **seven** and the numeral **7**, respectively.

- Three pictures or paper plates showing five, six and seven objects or counters, respectively.

Show seven fingers, with five fingers on one hand and two on the other.

Tell the child that,
- *When we can match something with this many fingers, we call it seven and use these names (**seven** and **7** are pointed to) for this many.*
- *As you look at seven, or these seven fingers, try to tell me something about the number seven.*

Some children quickly answer, *'I see a five and a two'*, or, *'I see five fingers and two thumbs'*, which demonstrates *flexible thinking* about numbers.

To further the idea about *flexible thinking* about numbers, or that numbers can have different names, ask the child,
- *Hold up as many as I am holding up and try to make your seven look different.*
- *What is different about your fingers and mine and what is the same?*

Present the pictures or paper plates and invite the child to,
- *Show, without counting, which of these has seven counters.*
- *Show, without counting, that the others do not have seven counters.*

Sevens – Where?

Possible Materials:

- Sketch of seven fingers.

- The numeral **7** and the word **seven** on little cards.

The child is requested to,
- *Try to think of when and where seven can be seen or used.*

If responses are not forthcoming, hints about the days in a week; about Snow-White; and the game Seven-Up could be presented.

If your parents or grandparents came from another country, ask them to write down what name they use or used for seven so we can check to see if these names for seven are in some way the same and how they might look different.

Buildings and Designs

- A box of building blocks of the same size.

- Pattern blocks or scrap pieces of coloured paper cut into different shapes.

- Several pieces of blank paper.

Place three pieces of paper in front of the child.
The child is requested to,
- *Select seven blocks for each piece of paper and try to build three houses that look different.*

Then invite the child to,
- *Select seven pattern blocks or seven scraps of coloured paper to design different looking flower beds for each of the houses you have built.*

At the end of the task, ask the child to suggest a name for the 'street' with the houses and the flower beds.

The child is asked to respond to,
- *How are the houses different?*
- *How are the gardens different?*
- *What things are the same for all the houses?*
- *What things are the same for all the flower beds?*
- *What is the same for the houses and the flower beds?*

Accommodating Responses

Sometimes redirection in questioning may be required to assist the child to reach a conclusion that indicates that, *'The same number can look different';* that is, the colours, shapes, sizes and the arrangements of the objects may differ for the same *cardinal number*(s).

Near Seven

Possible Materials:

- Fingers or cut-out of fingers.

After the other numbers have been introduced, hold up seven fingers. Invite the child to show with fingers and name the numbers as responses to:
- *a number less than seven and far away from seven.*
- *a number close to seven.*
- *a number greater than seven and close to seven.*
- *a number two away from seven.*

Many Different Ways

Possible Materials:

- Sketches of five pairs of balloons tied together.

- Or, five pieces of paper folded in half.

- A bunch of happy faces or counters.

The child is requested to,
- *Decorate each pair of balloons with seven happy faces.*
- *How can you put seven happy faces on two balloons?*
- *Try to think of all the different ways.*

- *Do you think there are more ways?*
- *Why. or why not?*

The problem can easily be changed to either placing seven counters or cookies on two parts of a cookie tray; placing cutouts of seven dwarfs on two benches or around two tables; or having a group of children act out the different possibilities for standing in two groups while stick people sketches are made to keep a record.

A summary for the setting should lead to and show the conclusion that: *'seven can look different'*:

It can be: *'five and two'*;
            'four and three';
            'one and six';
            'zero and seven.'

This conclusion is an important aspect of *flexible thinking* about number and necessary for developing *strategies* for the *basic addition facts*. However, at this point these summaries are not discussed in terms of addition.

Some children enjoy the challenge and extension to,
- *What could we do if we had seven happy faces and groups of three balloons, or seven cookies and a cookie tray with three parts?*
- *Try it and make sketches to show the different ways that you can find to show seven.*

As the other *cardinal numbers* are dealt with in similar problem solving settings, possible contexts can include putting fish cut-outs into fish tanks, or putting toy animals into pens.

Missing Parts

Possible Materials:

- A sketch of seven kites, or seven birds, or seven airplanes.

- A piece of non-transparent paper cut in the shape of a cloud.

- Fingers or sketches of fingers.

This type of an activity aids the development of *visualization* skills.

The child is requested to,
- *Show without counting that there are seven kites.*

While the child looks away, the cloud moves in and covers some of the kites.
- *How many do you think are behind the cloud?*
- *How do you know?*
- *Explain your thinking.*

Each time the child is asked to look away, the cloud hides a different number of kites.

Seven or fewer fingers are briefly shown.
For each display, the child is requested to,
- *Hold up the missing fingers that you think it would take to show seven.*

After each turn, hold up the flashed fingers again to check and see that all of the fingers show a seven.

Imagining – Going to Ten

Possible Materials:

- Fingers or cut-out of fingers.

Make the following requests after briefly showing several fingers,
- *How many did you see?*
- *Show with fingers how many more you think it takes to show ten or to go to ten.*
- *Use the word 'and' to tell the names for both numbers (i.e., seven and three).*

Repeat the procedure for different combinations of flashed fingers or numbers.

A simple variation of this task consists of asking the child to name and copy a number of fingers that is shown and to place the fingers onto the table while bending the remaining fingers.
- *How many fingers do you see or are shown?*
- *How many are not shown?*

About Numbers

Possible Materials:

- Three paper plates or three pieces of paper with six, seven, and eight dots or counters, respectively.

- The numerals **0** to **10** on little pieces of paper or cards.

For an *open-ended* task, show seven fingers.
Present the following prompts to the child,

- *Hold up as many fingers, find as many counters and place them onto a piece of paper.*
- *What are the two numbers next to and close to seven?*
- *Find six counters and place these onto a piece of paper and then find eight counters and put these onto a piece of paper.*

- *Look at the numbers six, seven, and eight. Move the counters for each number around.*
- *Try to show rows of counters. Is there anything you notice about these numbers?*
- *Is there anything that you can do with six and eight that cannot be done with seven?*

If the child notices that six and eight can be arranged in two rows with the same number in each row, and this is not possible with seven, ask the child to try and find other numbers that can be shown in two 'equal' rows and match each of these numbers with its number name. Tell the child that these numbers are called *even numbers* and the others are called *odd numbers*.

If a child does not recognize the property, present the task again at a later date.

Record Sheet Suggestions

As children learn about *numbers*, it is desirable to collect as many indicators of the development of *number sense* as possible. At this point the key indicators of *number sense* include aspects of *visualization* and *flexible thinking* about numbers.

1. Visualizing: Examples of recognizing number as a common attribute of sets – ***Houses and Rooms; Different Looking Fives; Differences Aside; Buildings and Designs***.

    _____

    _____

2. *Visualizing*: Examples of not being distracted by colour, shape, size or arrangement when examining or comparing sets on the basis of number – ***Houses and Rooms; Different Looking Fives; Differences Aside; Buildings and Designs***.

    _____

    _____

3. *Recognizing*: Examples of arrangements of numbers recognized without counting – ***Finger Flash***. _____

    _____

4. *Flexible thinking*: Examples of numbers shown in different ways and how they were shown – ***Show and Change***; ***About Seven***; ***Many Different Ways***.

    _____

    _____

5. *Recognizing* and *Visualizing*: Examples of responses to questions: *How many did you see?* and, *How many did you not see?* – ***Imagine***; ***Missing Parts***; ***Imagining*** – ***Going to Ten***.

    _____

    _____

6. *Relating:* Examples of terminology that are indicators of *relating* numbers – ***Greater Than and Less Than; Near Seven***. _____

    _____

7. *Visualizing:* Indicators of knowing *even* and *odd* – ***About Numbers***. _____

    _____

8. Indicators of *confidence* and *willingness to take risks*. _____

    _____

Rational Counting

Many young children have been taught something about *counting* very early in their lives. Some seem to enjoy the recital of number names. Anyone who has had conversations with these very young children knows that it is not difficult to discover indicators which show that this recital of number names is *rote*.

Examples of such indicators include such demonstrations as: assigning number names to spaces as well as to the objects that are counted; assigning two number names to one object and continuing to count beyond the objects that are to be counted.

As many young children count and point to objects while they utter *number names*, it is unlikely that they realize that the last *number name* they utter tells them how many objects are in the collection up to that point. For young children this procedure simply involves trying to *match* a *number name* with an object, nothing more.

When children are requested to stop while they are reciting *number names* or *counting orally* and are then asked, *What number name comes next?* many children are able to do so.

When the question, *Why?* is posed, the answers are somewhat predictable, and very likely to be incorrect: '*Because.*'; '*My mommy told me.*'; '*That's how it goes.*'; '*I have always knowed* (sic) *it.*'

The activities and settings show how the *mental strategies* involved with *ordering* and thinking about *patterns* are prerequisites for *rational counting* or counting with understanding.

Specific Goals for Rational Counting

Children will be able to:
- refer to *matching* as part of an explanation for what comes next in *growing patterns* with *numbers*.
- refer to *matching* as part of an explanation identifying hidden members of *growing patterns* with *numbers*.
- *match* members of *growing patterns* with *numbers* with the appropriate *number names*.
- refer to *cardinal number* as part of an explanation for what comes next in *growing patterns* recorded with *numerals*.
- refer to *cardinal number* as part of an explanation for how hidden members in *growing patterns* with *numerals* were identified.
- explain that in order for counting to give the answer to, *How many?*, the *number names* have to be stated in the correct *order*, starting with *'one'*, and each *number name* has to be *matched* with an object.
- demonstrate and explain that *counting* can start with any object in a collection of objects and carry on in any direction as long as *number names* are correctly *matched* with objects.
- use terms like *greater than*, *less than*, *close to*, *between*, and *far apart* when comparing and relating number names to one another.

Next Number Please

Possible Materials:

- Three paper plates in a row with one, two, and three counters, respectively.

Or, three pieces of paper showing the numbers.

Accommodating Responses

Ask the child to look at the dots and respond to,
- *What number do you think comes next?*
- *Why did you say that?*
- *Explain your thinking.*

Make the task more *open-ended* by inserting *could* into the question and requesting,
- *What do you think could come next?*
- *Explain why you think that number could come next.*

If only one response is volunteered, challenge the child with,
- *Do you think anything else could come next? Why?* or, *Why not?*

Accommodating Questions with Multiple Solutions

Many responses are possible. What possible reasons could children give for choosing: one counter [*]; two counters [**]; or three counters [***] for their next choice?

No doubt children come up with other choices, since *flexible thinking* and *risk taking* are encouraged for previous activities, and that includes tasks for *thinking about patterns*.

Questions with multiple solutions and interpretations carry some important messages. Great care needs to be taken when giving instructions for a desired response. Even then, an unexpected response may still be based on logical reasoning. Without asking the child, a wrong guess about the reason for the answer is possible.

Since many responses are possible for the question, *What comes next?,* generating assessment items that involve *patterns* with objects, numbers and numerals requires great care. The instructions for eliciting one required response for questions about patterns have to be specific and sometimes lengthy. It is all too easy to be negligent or a little careless and as a result, children may be treated unfairly. We need to ask,
- *How did you get that?* or,
- *Why did you say that?*

rather than marking answers as right or wrong.

If a *growing pattern* has not been part of the discussion at this point, ask the child to consider *growing* or *putting more* chips on a piece of paper.
- *How many chips do you think would go on the next piece of paper?*
- *Why?*

The explanation of *matching* the chips to the previous card and then putting down one more chip as we go on to the next card is presented. If this *growing pattern* continues,
- *What comes next?*

Before and Next Please

Possible Materials:

• One set of cards, envelopes or paper plates with the number names from **0** to **10**.

• One set of cards or envelopes showing the numbers zero to ten.

Cards are selected to show the following *growing pattern*:

[ ] [3] [5] [7] [ ]

The number one [*] is shown on the back of the first blank card, and the number nine [*********] on the back of the last card

Tell the child that the pattern is a *growing pattern* and ask,
- *How many dots do you think are drawn on the next card?*
- *How do you know? Explain how you got your answer.*
- *Let's turn the card over to see if you were right.*

If the *growing pattern* is correctly identified, ask for predictions for the next card and the first card in the sequence.

If the response is different from the one shown on the card that was turned over, ask the child,
- *How do you think it is possible to get this number as an answer?*

After the pattern has been successfully identified by making reference to *matching and two more*, invite the child to,
- *Place the correct number name below each number.*

Use the same questioning strategy and procedure for the following *growing patterns*:

[ ] [2] [4] [6] [ ]   and   [ ] [3] [4] [5] [ ]

For the first *pattern* the *numbers* for zero [ ] and eight [*******] and for the second *pattern* the *numbers* for two [**] and six [******] appear on the backside of the blank cards, respectively.

Missing Number Names

Materials:

- Eleven cards or envelopes showing the numerals **0** to **10**, respectively.

- Counters.

Some cards are turned over for the following *growing pattern*:

[ ] [4] [5] [ ] [7] [8] [ ]

The child is invited to,
- *Think of a growing pattern.*
- *What number names do you think are on the cards that are turned over?*

Follow correct responses with,
- *How did you know?*
- *Explain your thinking.*

If the answers are not correct, use counters to construct the *growing pattern*.

Use the same questioning strategy and procedure for the following *growing patterns*:

[ ] [3] [5] [ ] [9]   and   **[2] [4] [ ] [8] [ ]**

Accommodating Responses

During diagnostic interviews, some children in grade one and a few in grade two insisted that the growing pattern: **[2] – [4] – [6] – [ ]**, *'Is not possible because there have to be numbers between two and four and between four and six.'*

It is very likely that these children missed out on first building *patterns* with *numbers*, then with *numbers* and *number names*, and finally with *number names*. It could be that many or most of their experiences were at the symbolic level, looking at numerals rather than numbers and numerals. They lacked the ability to *visualize*, or did not 'see' the numbers 'connected' to the *number names*. It is likely that these children will benefit from further activities that involve growing patterns with numbers and growing patterns with numbers and numerals.

Give It a Try

Materials:

- Two sets of eleven cards showing the numerals **0** to **10**, respectively.

The child is faced with the sequence:

[1] [2] [3] [ ] [ ] [ ]

and the two sets of cards with all of the numerals.

For a very *open-ended* task, challenge the child with,
- *Think about patterns.*
- *Try and think of all the possible number names that you think could come next.*

Accommodating Responses

For each response, try to guess what the child is thinking and then test the guess with another numeral. Record all generated *patterns*. Ask the child to sort these recordings into *repeating* or *growing patterns*.

The responses for, *What could come next?* that have been collected from children over the years include **0, 1, 2, 3, 4, 5, 6, 8** and **10**.

There have been others not included in the list because the child did not explain a *pattern* with the *numeral*.

As one can surmise, a child will be encountered who will justify the usage of a *numeral* with, '*Because*.'

Then there are always surprises. One young boy placed a **6** as the next numeral. For obvious reasons this can make an observer curious, because it looks as if an advanced type of addition might be involved.

However, the boy answered the question, *Why did you put down a six?* Emphatically with, '*I am six years old*' – a very important number for him.

The response to, *What would you put down next?* was, '*One*', and on he went to build a repeating pattern.

This is another example that illustrates that without asking questions at certain times, conclusions can be reached that are incorrect.

What's Wrong

Materials:

• Counters.

Invite the child to watch as the counters are counted incorrectly.
- *Watch and tell me when you see or hear something that you think is done incorrectly.*
- *Explain why you think it is wrong.*

As objects are counted, make the following errors:
- Spaces between objects are assigned *number names.*
- Objects are assigned two *number names.*
- Continue counting beyond the last object in the set.
- In a circular or triangular arrangement of objects, ignore the starting point and continue the counting..
- Recite the *number names* in an incorrect order.
- Skip one *number name.*
- Repeat one *number name.*

After reacting to the incorrect ways of counting, challenge the child with,
- *Try to make up your own rule for counting correctly that you can share with a younger child.*
- *What part of your rule do you think is important to remember?*
- *Why do you think that is the case?*

Start Again

Materials:

• Counters.

Place eight counters in front of the child.

The child is invited to,
- *Count the chips several times.*
- *Each time you count start with a different object.*

Upon completion of the task pose the following questions,
- *What was different about your ways of counting?*
- *What was the same about each time you counted?*
- *What can you tell somebody about counting and starting points?*

Find the Sad Face

Materials:

• Paper plates
that show ten happy faces
and one sad face.

The number [******] and numeral for **six** [6] are recorded on the back of the sad face. The remaining numbers as well as numerals from **zero** to **ten** are recorded on the back of the happy faces, respectively. Pieces of paper with instructions or hints about finding the *number* on the plate which hides the sad face: **It is not behind five; It is behind a number greater than one; It is behind a number less than nine; It is behind a number greater than three and less than eight; It is behind a number close to seven.**

Randomly select six of the paper plates and present these to the child with the *numbers* and *numerals* face up. Invite the child to,
• *Order the numbers from least to greatest.*

Present the remaining paper plates, one at a time, with the requests,
• *Place the number into the ordered sequence where you think it belongs.*
• *How do you know it belongs there?*
• *Explain your thinking.*

After this task is completed, tell the child,
• *Behind one of the paper plates is a sad face and behind the others are happy faces.*
• *The challenge is to try and find the sad face by following instructions.*

The first instruction about the sad face is presented: **It is not behind five.** The child is requested to,
• *Point to several paper plates that you think could hide the sad face.*
• *Explain your answer.*
• *Now point to one paper plate that could not hide the sad face.*
• *Turn it over to see if you are right.*

These types of questions are repeated after each new hint about a *number* is presented:
- **It is behind a number greater than one.**
- **It is behind a number less than nine.**
- **It is behind a number greater than three and less than eight.**
- **It is behind a number close to seven.**

Ask the child to look at and think about all of the hints and respond to,
• *Which hint do you think gave you the most information about where the sad face was hidden?*
• *Why do you think that is the case?*
• *Which hint gave you little information?*
• *Why is that the case?*

Find the Penny

Materials:

- Eleven envelopes with the numerals **0** to **10**, respectively.

- A penny.

Pieces of paper with the instructions about the *number name* on the envelope with the hidden penny:
- **It is not between 3 and 5**;
- **It is not between 7 and 9**;
- **It is greater than 3**;
- **It is greater than 5**;
- **It is less than 10**;
- **It is less than 9**;
- **It is not 6**.

Randomly select and present the child with six of the envelopes. Make the request,
- *Order these from least to greatest.*

Present the remaining envelopes, one at a time, with the request,
- *Place the envelope into the ordered sequence where you think it belongs.*
- *How do you know it belongs there?*

While the child looks away, place a penny into the envelope with the numeral **7**.

Present the first instruction about the number name on the envelope with the hidden penny:
> **It is not between 3 and 5.**

Invite the child to,
- *Give the number names of several envelopes that you think could contain the penny.*
- *Name the envelope that could not contain the penny.*
- *Turn this envelope over.*

Repeat these types of requests and questions after each new hint about a *number name* is presented:
- **It is not between 7 and 9.**
- **It is greater than 3.**
- **It is greater than 5.**
- **It is less than 10.**
- **It is less than 9.**
- **It is not 6.**

A Riddle

Possible Materials:

- Eleven envelopes with the numerals **0** to **10**, respectively.

- A penny.

- A chart or a piece of paper showing:
  The Number
  - is close to;
  - is between;
  - is not between;
  - is not;
  - is greater than;
  - is less than.

Accommodating Responses

The ability to *communicate mathematically* implies that mathematical terminology is used orally as well as written.

Creating a riddle invites the child to think, and provides an opportunity to *think about thinking.*

It is assumed that asking the child to create and write instructions for finding coin in a secret envelope should be done after the child has solved riddles like those suggested for,
Find the Sad Face and **Find the Penny.**

Invite the child to place a penny into one of the envelopes and to,
- *Write instructions to help a friend try to find the penny.*
- *Use some of the words from the chart.*

The task encourages young children to *think* about *numbers and number names.* An examination of the instructions created by a child provides opportunities for the child to reflect, modify and expand on the information provided. Use questions to have the child clarify thinking and to provide more information, but it may take time and several attempts in order for the child to articulate hints, the writing to improve and hints to increase in specificity.

The first sentence ever written by one boy about a secret number was, *'I like ten'* and his comment, *'Guess my number'* still elicits smiles as this very first and somewhat unusual attempt at writing instructions about a number.

There are young children who show surprise when an adult is unable to guess the *number name* they have written about. How can that be? They have written the instructions and they know what the number name is, why wouldn't someone who is much older know?

This was the case for this example,
'It is clos (sic) *to ten and it is how old my Brudr* (sic) *is.'*
Somewhat reluctantly the student provided more hints.

Printing Numerals
or
Number Names

The development of *number sense* and the ability to *count rationally* does not in any way depend upon the ability to print or write numerals, nor the ability to print these neatly.

Learning how to print the number names should be part of printing lessons rather than mathematics learning.

There are children, and that is especially true for young boys, who reverse numerals or produce scribbles for some numerals that are difficult to recognize. This lack of fine motor control is not an indicator of lack of *number sense*. For the majority of children, reversal difficulties disappear over time.

Some children can be helped with activities that involve reversing on purpose, or using a model to identify correctly printed numerals and trying to explain what was done to obtain the incorrect examples.

Ordinal Numerals

Once children have some familiarity with methods of establishing order among *numbers* and *numerals*, they can engage in activities in which *ordinal names* such as *first*, *last*, *second*, *third,* and so on, occur.

Introduce these names in simple one-dimensional situations. From there children move on to thinking about sequences within sequences, and this can be extended to activities involving coordinate planes.

Specific Goals for Ordinal Numerals

Children will be able to:
- use the language of order to label objects according to their position: i.e., *number one* or *first*, *number two* or *second*.
- recognize that labelling and identifying order is independent of direction; it can begin anywhere.
- recognize a special property when the order of an odd number of objects is reversed; the object in the middle holds the same position.
- apply order within an ordered sequence: i.e., the first and second boy in a line-up of children.

Order Please

Possible Materials:

- Six toy animals
  or
  different cars.

To introduce *ordinal numeral* invite the child to,
- *Name the animal that is number one or first.*
- *Name the animal that is number two or second.*
- *Name the animal that is number three or third.*
- *Name the animal that is number six, sixth or last.*

- *Have you ever heard someone use the words first, second, third, ...?*
- *Who used the words?*
- *Where and when?*

The child looks at six objects in a row facing in one direction.
As an object is pointed to, in random order, the child is invited to,
- *Name the place of the animal in the row in two ways.*

For example, *'The dog is number two or second.'*

Second Order

Possible Materials:

- Several of two kinds
  of plastic animals,
  people or cars.

The animals alternate and face in the same direction.
For Example:

    cow – horse – cow – horse – cow – horse – cow – horse – cow

The child is requested to:
- *Point to the animal that is first, second, fourth, sixth, and so forth.*
- *Point to the horse that is first, second, third and fourth.*
- *Try to point to: the second horse;*
                   the fourth cow;
                   the fourth horse.

The Other Way

Possible Materials:

- Five toy cars or animals
  in a row facing
  the same direction.

The requests to the child include,
- *Point to the car that is first (second, third, fourth and fifth).*

- *Turn the cars around and make them face the other way.*
- *Now point to the car that is first (second, third, fourth and fifth) now.*

- *What is different about the cars now?*
- *Did you notice anything that is the same or special?*

If the child notices that one car kept the same position, turn the animals around from the previous task and this discovery could be tested.

For further tests of the discovery:
  three objects;   four objects;   six objects;   seven objects
in a row facing the same direction are presented.

- *For which of these sequences is it true that one object keeps the same position when the objects face in the opposite direction?*
- *Why do you think that is the case?*

Is It? – It Is!

Possible Materials:

- Three rows of five different toy animals or toy cars all facing in the same direction.

One row is close to the child and the other rows are farther away.

For a *Name the Animal* setting, describe a position and invite the child to identify the correct animal.

After labelling the rows *first*, *second* and *third* row, make a request to name the animals in the following positions:
- *First row and fourth animal.*
- *Third row and second animal.*
- *Second row and first animal.*
- *Fifth animal in the third row.*
- *Fourth animal in the second row.*

For a *Name the Place or Position* setting, point to an animal and ask the child to use ordinals for the row and the place in the row to identify its position.

After rearranging all of the animals to face in the opposite direction, ask the child,
- *Which animals are still in the same positions?*
- *Why is that the case?*

Tell the child,
- *If [(1,2) is pointed to] identifies row one or the first row and animal two or the second animal in it, which animal is it?*

Present each ordinal number pair, one at a time:
  (2,2) (2,5) (3,4) (4,3) (5,5)

Ask the child,
- *Which animal do you think is identified?*
- *Explain your thinking.*

Point to an animal. Invite the child to use number names for the row and the place in the row to identify and record its position.

Read each recording in two ways.
For example: **(1,3)** is read as,
  'Row one, animal number three' and, *'First row, the third animal.'*

Record Sheet Suggestions

The main goal is to collect data about the ability to *count rationally* or with *understanding*.
How does the child demonstrate *what comes next* and *why* for different patterns:
    with numbers; with numbers and numerals; and with numerals?

1. Explanations for predicting the next number for
    growing patterns with numbers – ***Next Number Please***. _____
    _____

2. Explanations for predicting hidden members in
    growing patterns with numbers – ***Before and Next***. _____
    _____

3. Explanations for predicting the next numeral for *growing*
    patterns with numerals – ***Missing Number Names***. _____
    _____

4. Explanations for predicting a hidden numeral for
    growing patterns with numerals – ***Give It A Try***. _____
    _____

5. Explanations for what is meant by *counting*
    correctly – ***What's Wrong*** and ***Start Again***. _____
    _____

6. Indicators of understanding that *counting*
    can be done in any direction – ***Start Again***. _____
    _____

7. Indicators of *confidence* and *willingness to take risks*. _____
    _____

Numbers for Two-Digit Numerals

The *general* and *specific goals* for numbers for two-digit numerals are similar to the goals for the numbers and numerals to nine.

The focus is to foster the development of *number sense* and accommodating its components:
- *visualizing;*
- *recognizing;*
- *thinking flexibly;*
- *estimating;*
- *connecting;*
- *relating.*

Since *number sense* is the foundation for *numeracy*, a requisite for success with mathematics, it is advantageous to state the *key specific goals* for each of the *components* of *number sense* again.

**Specific Goals
for
Numbers for
Two-Digit Numerals
and
Number Sense**

Children will be able to:
- explain how parts of manipulative materials illustrate the meanings of the digits for stated number names.
- describe the answer for, *How many?* for a given number without counting every object.
- use manipulative materials to illustrate how numbers can be shown in different ways and can have different names.
- use ten as a *referent* to arrive at an estimate to the nearest ten, *about _ tens,* for a given number of objects.
- use appropriate comparison language to explain how numbers and numerals *relate* to one another.

10 – A Special Numeral

Possible Materials:

- Pictures of six pairs of balloons tied together, or six pieces of paper each separated into halves.

- The numeral **10** on a card.

- A box of happy faces or counters, or a pen for drawing dots.

This task shows the child that there is something very special about the numeral **10**.

The goal for the first part is to show that ten can have many different names. The happy faces, or counters as cookies on trays; or drawn dots show that ten objects can be shown in two parts in different ways.

The child faces several pairs of pictures of balloons.
Make the requests to,
- *Find ten happy faces and put these in some way onto the two balloons.*
- *Look at the two balloons and tell something about the number ten.*

Repeat the following request,
- *Now think of a different way of showing ten happy faces on two balloons.*

After each attempt record the number name for ten below each pair of balloons.
For example: **6 and 4**; **7 and 3**; **8 and 2**; **9 and 1**.

After several examples ask the child,
- *How do you think the pairs of balloons are different?*
- *What is the same for each pair?*
The last question may need to be repeated before *'ten'* becomes part of the answer.

Hold up ten fingers and make an *open-ended* invitation,
- *Look at these ten fingers.*
- *Tell me everything you can about ten just from looking at the fingers.*
If a child looks puzzled, hints about considering the two hands; each of the fingers; or the eight fingers and the two thumbs are provided.

Place ten fingers onto the table alongside the *numeral* **10**.
Tell the child,
- *Whenever we see this number name, there is a special way to think about it.*
- *When we see this number name, we say **ten**, but it would be better if we would say **one ten zero** and think of it as **one person holding up all the fingers** or as **one group of ten**.*

To show that the child remembers, make the request to read this *numeral*, for a while at least, in two different ways. The advantage and the possible contribution this method of reading makes to developing *number sense* becomes obvious in the next section.

Look and Tell

Possible Materials:

• Cards with sketches of combinations of hands and fingers to show the numbers between **10** and **20**.

• Rather than cards, digital photos of children holding up fingers to show these numbers could be used.

• Cards with the numerals **11** to **19**.

• Cards with word names for the numbers **eleven** to **nineteen**.

The child is asked to look at a sketch, or a digital photo of the children holding up fingers and respond to,
  • *Tell me everything you can about the number of fingers you see?*
  • *What numbers come to mind when you look at these fingers?*

Provide cues so that the child thinks about fingers and thumbs.
For example, *fourteen fingers* can be thought of as:
  - *two fives and four more.*
  - *twelve fingers and two thumbs* or, *eleven fingers and three thumbs.*
  - *one ten and four more.*

Tell the child that when we see these (fourteen) fingers we say, **one child is holding up ten** and there are **four more**, or, **one group of ten** and **four more**, or, **fourteen**, *and we print the number name* **14**, *where the* **1** *tells us that* **there is one group of ten**, *and the* **4** *tells us that* **there are four more**. Invite the child to read the number name in two ways, as **one ten four** and **fourteen**.

The same procedure is used for other numbers and number names between ten and twenty.

Assigning different names to numbers and reading the numeral in two ways fosters *flexible thinking* about a number as well as *visualization*.

The reading in two ways helps avoid confusion about two-digit number names. For some children rote learning about number names leads to confusion, especially for some of the *teen* numerals. Reversal problems occur for these children. For example, they will record **41** when **14** is called for, or vice versa; or will read **14** as *'forty-one.'* This is an indicator of a lack of *visualization*, a key component of *number sense*.

The reading of the numerals in two ways can help prevent this problem.

Order and Guess

Possible Materials:

- Cards or digital photos of pairs of children using their fingers to show the numbers for **11** to **19**.

- Cards with the numerals for **11** to **19**.

Present numbers in random order, one at a time, and ask the child,
- *What numbers do you see?*
- *What are two ways of answering,*
- *How many fingers are there?*

A few examples of the answers may be necessary at the start of this activity..

After the shuffled cards with the numerals are presented, the following requests are made,
- *Put the number names in order.*
- *How do you know the order is correct? Explain your thinking.*

While the child looks away, turn the ordered numerals face down. Invite the child to,
- *Try and find sixteen.*
- *How did you decide where to look? Explain your thinking.*
- *Where would thirteen be? See if you are right.*

One Will Fly

Possible Materials:

- Sketch of nine balloons in a row tied to a horizontal string labelled with the numerals **11** to **19**, respectively.

- Stacked instruction cards about one balloon that will fly away.

The number on the balloon:
- **is less than 17**;
- **is greater than 13**;
- **is even**;
- **is close to 17**.

Solving and writing riddles about number names provides opportunities to relate numbers as well as for reflection.
- *Find the number name on the balloon that will fly away.*

Present the hints in order, one at a time.
- *The balloon has a name for a number that:*
- **is less than 17**.
- **is greater than 13**.
- **is even**.
- **is close to 17**.

After each hint ask the child,
- *Which balloon(s) could be flying away?*
- *Which balloon(s) could not be flying away?*

Cover or turn over the answer or answers for the latter question.

Present an opportunity for further reflection that involves relating numbers when asking the child to think about one balloon and to write or give hints so it can be identified without giving away the answer.

Careful – Not True

Possible Materials:

• Twenty rectangles with the numerals **0** to **19**, respectively.

The task is to identify the secret door behind which a treasure (dime) is hidden.

Cards with instructions about the numeral on the door as listed below.

A different way of thinking is required when all of the instructions are ***not true***.

Tell the child,
- *Some of those who hide treasures sometimes do not want to tell the truth about where it is hidden. When they are asked where the treasure is hidden, they know that,*
All statements are false.

Present the instructions, one at a time.
After each ask the child,
- *What number name do you think it could not be?*
- *What number name do you think it could be?*

Show the answers for the second question by turning the door, or doors over.

A reminder about the statements not being true may be needed.

The rectangle or door that hides the treasure has a name for a number that:
- **is even.**
- **is greater than fifteen.**
- **can be found by starting at zero and skip-counting by three.**
- **is less than the number of fingers on both hands.**
- **is greater than one dozen.**

A request to write or make up a riddle about a name for a number where all of the statements are false is quite a challenge for a child.

For an initial task reduce the range of the numbers to be considered.

It is advantageous for children to try this in pairs, since they can remind each other about the things that need to be kept in mind.

How Many? – Find Out and Show

Possible Materials:

- **32** toothpicks.

- Rubber bands.

- Card showing the numeral **32**.

Place thirty-two toothpicks in front of the child.
Invite the child to,
- *Try and think of some possible ways of counting the toothpicks to find the answer to how many toothpicks?*
Yes, there are different ways to count these to find the answer to, *How many?*

There are times when telling is part of mathematics learning.
Tell the child, *there is a way of counting that* involves *putting objects into **groups of ten** and we do this as often as we can. Then we record how many **groups of ten** there are and how many are left over, or how many left over 'ones.'*

Illustrate the method with the toothpicks. Use a rubber band or a twist tie to bundle each group of ten.
- We have *three groups of ten* and *two left over 'ones.'*

Show the **32** and point to the appropriate digits as the numeral is read as, ***three tens*** and ***two ones*** and ***thirty two***.

To foster *visualization* of the number behind the number name, present the following challenge,
- *Try to think of the fewest number of children we would need to show the number for thirty-two with fingers and how would these children do it?*

- *What do you think would be the greatest number of children needed to show thirty-two with fingers?*

- *Do you think there are other ways of showing thirty-two using the fingers of children? Explain your thinking*

Look, Tell and Think

Possible Materials:

- Sketch,
or a digital photo,
of three children holding
up fingers.

Two children
are holding up ten fingers
and one child is holding
up four fingers.

Invite the child to,
- *Look at the fingers held up by the children and without counting, say something about the number shown with all of the fingers.*
- *What else can you see and say about the number?*

If responses are not forthcoming, ask the child,
- *How many tens or groups of ten do you see and how many more?*
- *How many fives do you see and how many more?*

Record the numeral **24** as the answer to, *how many fingers are being held up?*

Ask the child to read the numeral in two different ways,
'two tens and four ones' and, *'twenty four.'*

An opportunity to consider the meanings of the number names
is provided by asking children,
- *Why do you think it would not make sense to say, 'two-four' for this number?*

The child is invited to,
- *Look at the children and say the number name.*

- *How many do you think would there be if another child joined these children and held up ten fingers? If this child used any number of fingers, other than ten, what are the possible numbers that could be shown? Explain your thinking.*

- *How many do you think would there be if one of the two children sat down?*
- *Is another answer possible? Explain your thinking.*

- *How many would there be if one more finger would be held up?*

- *How many would there be if one finger was taken down?*

If the child cannot visualize the new numbers for these questions,
simulate the suggested actions or use sketches to show the answers.

Different, But the Same

Possible Materials:

- Sketches
or digital photos
of two groups of children.

In one group,
two children are holding
up ten fingers each,
and one child holds
up one finger.

In the other group,
one child holds
up ten fingers
and eleven children hold
up one finger each.

- Toothpicks and rubber bands.

Invite the child to,
- *Look at the two sketches of children and say something about how they are different.*
- *Do you think there is anything the same about the two sketches?*

To provide a focus, ask the child,
- *How many fingers are held up in each group of children?*

After the child has determined that there are twenty-one fingers in each group, ask the child,
- *How are the ways of showing twenty-one different?*

Illustrate the two ways of showing the number with toothpicks:
- one bundle of ten and eleven singles, and
- two bundles of ten and one single toothpick.

Prompt the child to,
- *Use toothpicks and show: thirteen (twenty-five; thirty-two) in two different ways.*

Name, Show and More

Materials:

- Cards
showing the numerals:
13 – 24 – 25 – 31 – 36
– 42 – 52 – 63.

Randomly select a card and make the request,
- *Tell how many groups of ten there are in the number.*

The cards are placed in random order in front of the child:
- *Point to the number name with the greatest number of tens.*
- *Point to the number name with the least number of tens.*
- *Point to two with the same number of tens.*
- *Point to the number names that could be shown using the fingers of four children.*

As a number name is pointed to, make the request,
- *Indicate by showing fingers, the fewest number of children it would take to show that number name with fingers.*

Invite the child to,
- *Order the number names from least to greatest.*

Point to a number name and invite the child to,
- *State the name for a number that is ten greater than this number name.*
- *State the name of the number that is ten less than this number name.*
- *Why do you think there is more than one correct answer for the requests: to state a number name that comes after this number name and state a number name that comes before this number name?*

About 'About'

Possible Materials:

• A paper plate with forty-two counters, pennies or toothpicks that is covered with a piece of paper.

• Three separate pieces of paper showing one of:
About two tens or 20;
About four tens or 40;
About six tens or 60.

Accommodating Responses

Invite the child to look at the plate. Remove the cover and ask,

• *Look at your ten fingers and then at the counters.*

• *If you were to put all of the pennies into groups of ten, about how many groups of ten do you think you could make?*
Pick one of these: **About two tens or 20**
                                    About four tens or 40
                                    About six tens or 60

• *Tell why you chose it. Explain your thinking.*

The use of the ten fingers as a *referent* is one example that illustrates to the child what we mean by *estimating* and how it differs from guessing.

If a child uses ten as a *referent* and pretends to group the counters, any response is considered appropriate because such a response is indicative of the child's *sense of number* at that particular moment.

There exists no need to count the counters and attempt to make some sort of comparison. What possible purpose does this serve? At worst, it might discourage the child from attempting any future task involving estimation.

If by chance, an answer is judged to be inappropriate, then provide more opportunities to make predictions about a numbers of objects and putting these into groups of ten as well, alter the choices for possible responses.

In terms of a hierarchy of tasks, initially present only two choices that are quite far apart – **About four tens or 40** and **About nine tens or 90.**

Then reduce the range – **About four tens or 40** and **About six tens or 60.** As more estimation tasks are presented, the range for the three choices can be reduced.

A modification to these types of settings consists of presenting two paper plates to a child, i.e., one with **42** counters and one with **82** counters. Make the following requests,

• *Look at your ten fingers.*
• *Which of the plates do you think holds about four tens or forty counters?*
• *If that plate* (the selected choice is pointed to) *holds about four tens or forty counters, about how many counters do you think are on the other plate?*
• *Explain how you decided on your answer.*

Pick the Winner

Possible Materials:

• A sketch of
thirty things in three rows:
race cars;
stick people with a place
to record a numeral;
airplanes.

• Or,
happy faces in three rows
labeled with the numerals
60 to **89**.

• Cards with instructions
about how to identify
the winner – as listed below.

• Or,
part of a number line
from **60** to **89**.

Present hints, one at a time, for identifying the number name on the winning car, or trying to find the secret number name on the number line.

After each hint, ask the following questions,
• *Which car or cars could be the winner?* or,
What numbers are possible?

• *Which car or cars could not be the winner?* or,
Which numbers could be covered or crossed out?

The cars or number names that are ruled out are covered with a chip or a piece of paper.

The car that won the race has a name for a number that:
- **does not have a 5 in it.**
- **is greater than 62.**
- **is less than 86.**
- **is not between 62 and 65.**
- **is not between 80 and 85.**
- **does not have a 6, 7, 8, or 9 in the ones place.**
- **does not have a 0, 1, or 2 in the ones place.**
- **is an even number.**

The terminology used for the instructions depends on the words a child is familiar with and are modified accordingly.

A list of terms the child is familiar with is printed out and the request to create a riddle about a car or a number on the number line is made.

Record Sheet Suggestions

As children talk and write about *numbers* and *numerals*, it is important to listen and look for possible indicators of *number sense*. Record these indicators as they provide information about the development of this important aspect of mathematics learning.

1. *Visualization:* Explanations that show that ten can be thought of as a special number name, **10 – A Special Numeral**. _____

   _____

2. *Visualization:* Explanation that states a reason for reading two-digit number names in two ways – **Look and Tell; Order and Guess;** and **How Many? – Find and Show.**

   _____

   _____

3. *Visualization:* Explanations indicative of thinking of numbers when listening to number names, looking at number names, or talking about number names – **Look, Tell and Think** and **Name, Show and More**. _____

   _____

4. *Recognizing:* Indicators that a displayed number can be named without counting each object – **Look, Tell and Think** and **Different, but the Same**. _____

   _____

5. *Flexible thinking:* Examples of representing numbers and naming number names in different ways or in at least two ways, using tens and ones – **Look, Tell and Think**.

   _____

   _____

6. *Estimating:* Explanation of a strategy used to find an answer for, *About how many tens are there? –* **About 'About'**. _____

   _____

7. *Relating:* Terms and phrases used when numbers and number names are compared – **One will Fly; Careful – Not True; Pick the Winner**. _____

   _____

8. *Connecting:* Examples of statements that indicate when and where numbers and number names are used. _____

   _____

9. Indicators of *confidence* and *willingness to take risks*. _____

   _____

Operations

Use mathematical statements **2 + 3** and **7 — 4** to describe physical situations of interest to young children. Initially, the major concern is with children's ability to associate certain events and situations in their everyday life with a mathematical description of the events. Focus on the child developing an understanding of the statements and not deriving or reciting answers.

At the early stages *operations* are best understood if children associate these operations with relevant actions. Thus *addition* is the act of combining things, while the most common interpretation of *subtraction* is the act of separating them. We want children to use their understanding of *number* and *number names* and along with the *symbols* for *addition* and *subtraction* to write and interpret *summaries* for such situations.

Young children can make sense, at an initial level, of events from their experiences that involve *multiplication* and the two types of *division*. Any setting that involves *one-to-many correspondence* can be used to introduce the action for multiplication. Children know how to assign members of a group, one at a time, to two or more teams and how to make-up as many teams of four as possible from a group. These two operations are beyond the scope of this book. Suffice it to say that *number sense* is the pre-requisite that serves children as they learn the *basic multiplication facts* and connect these to the *basic division facts*.

Children learn to write summaries for events and actions when they are simulated with counters for events described orally and when pictorial representations are used to show actions. Children also learn to interpret summaries by simulating the intended actions with counters, by creating appropriate stories, and by preparing sketches that show the intended actions.

At the introductory stage, when the focus is on identifying and interpreting the *actions,* rather than on being able to recite or record answers, it does not make any difference which of the two operations is introduced first. Both types of *actions* relate to children's experiences, and one is not more difficult to understand than the other.

However, when the focus is on writing *equations* and learning the *basic facts* the order of presentation is important. Since learning the *basic subtraction facts* involves not much more than *connecting* these facts to the *basic addition facts*, confidence with the latter is a necessary prerequisite. It is for this reason that most references for students deal with addition prior to subtraction.

(continued next page ...)

Operations (cont'd)

The introductions of addition and subtraction are discussed here at the same time simply for the sake of convenience.

Specific Goals for Introducing Addition and Subtraction

Children will be able to:

- identify words and phrases from their experiences that are indicative of the *additive* and *subtractive actions*.
- substitute *'plus'* or *'add'* for words that describe the *additive action* and *'minus'* or *'take away'* for words that describe *subtractive action*.
- use familiar and mathematical language to explain what the *symbols* + and − mean.
- use objects to simulate the *additive* and *subtractive* actions for events from their experiences and record *mathematical statements* to *summarize* the events.
- make up meaningful stories for *mathematical addition* and *subtraction statements* and dramatize or simulate the actions.
- select from choices of *mathematical statements* those that correctly describe the action in a diagram and provide reasons for the selection based on the *numbers* shown and the *action*.
- record *mathematical statements* for given diagrams and make up a story for the illustrated *action* and for the *numbers* that are shown.

'More' Stories

Possible Materials:

• Sketches
of two children (stick people)
in a doorway and
three children
are walking toward the door.

• Or, two birds on a branch
and three birds flying
toward the branch.
The movement
or action is indicated
with 'action' lines.

Student texts use such things as 'action lines', 'arrows' or a 'hand along with action lines' to indicate that children are to pretend that some sort of movement is taking place. This interpretation cannot be taken for granted. The meanings have to be explained as illustrated by the responses of two young children asked to suggest the meaning of the 'action lines.'

Their responses,
'The sheep are kicking up grass.'
'The spiders are making webs.'

Learning how to interpret pictorial representations that indicate actions involves three different aspects or levels of perception:
- recognition of the numbers.
- interpretation of the action.
- integration of the numbers and the action.

Tell a story that involves the *additive action*:
'Two children were at home and three more came to visit.
Ask the child to model the action with counters.

Invite the child to tell *action* stories about:
- *children playing on the playground and other
    children joining them.*
- *children coming to a field to fly kites.*
- *more fish being put into an aquarium.*
- *more children jumping into a swimming pool.*
- *getting more coins from someone.*
- *more birds landing on a branch.*

Simulate the action in each story with counters and use words
or phrases to describe the action such as:
- *more came;*
- *more joined them;*
- *came along;*
- *was given more;*
- *got some more.*

Summary Writing

Possible Materials:

- Sketch
of an aquarium
with three fish in it
and
two more being put into it.

- Or, three apples in a
basket
and a hand dropping
two more into the basket.

- Counters.

Tell a story about the fish,
> *There were three fish in the aquarium.*
> *We bought two more and put them into the aquarium.*

Tell the child, *the story can be summarized by printing **3 plus 2**, where:*
- *the **3** tells us how many fish were in the aquarium.*
- *the **plus** tells us about the action that took place and this word can be used in place of the action words that tell us about joining things and putting things together.*
- *the **2** tells us how many are put into the aquarium.*

Invite the child to,
- *Tell the whole story again and show what happens with counters.*

As you retell stories from the previous task *'More' Stories*, or tell new stories, record summaries using numerals and **plus**. After each recorded summary, make the requests,
- *Retell the story and point to each matching part of the summary.*
- *Show what happened in the story with counters.*

Which Summary?

Materials:

- Cards showing:
  [**4 plus 1**]
  [**5 plus 3**]
  [**2 plus 6**]
  [**1 plus 7**]
  [**0 plus 4**]

Invite the child to,
- *Think about one of the summaries and make up an action story from around the home or the playground.*

Request the child to,
- *Explain each part of the summary and show what happens with counters.*

Tell the child, *This sign [+] can be used for the word **plus** and this sign reminds us of all of the action words we have used.*

Invite the child to,
- *Use the new sign to write a summary for the story:*

There are three people in our house and four came to visit.
- *Tell me all of the words you can think of that describe the actions for the plus sign.*

Making Sketches and Summaries

Possible Materials:

- Sketches that indicate actions.

  For example:
  - 3 apples and
    4 being added.

  - 2 birds on a branch and
    1 more landing.

  - 4 pucks in a net and
  1 more being shot into the net.

- Pairs of cards with the
  following summaries:
  [4 + 3]
  [3 + 4]
  [2 + 1]
  [1 + 2]
  [4 + 1]
  [1 + 4]

Show the child the two cards showing **4 + 3** and **3 + 4** and ask:

- *Which of these do you think tells about the picture
  with the apples? How do you know?*

- *If you were to draw a picture for **4 + 3**, what would you draw?
  Explain your thinking.*

- *What does the first number name in a summary tell us?*

- *What does the second number name tell us?*

Use the same choice format for the other pairs of sketches.

After the child has made a choice and has explained the reason
for the choice, invite the child to,

- *Make up a story for the other choice.*

- *How is your story different from the one you were given?*

'Away' Stories

Possible Materials:

- Sketches of events showing the *subtractive action* with 'action lines':

  - three birds sitting on a branch and one flying away.

  - six balloons on strings in a hand and one flying away.

  - two of five apples on a table rolling off.

  - two planes on a runway and one taking off.

Invite the child to,
  - *Try to tell a story about what you think is happening in each sketch.*

After isolating the action words, ask the child to think of other words that describe similar actions:

separating;
going away or *leaving behind;*
lost some;
dropped some;
some were left behind;
some were taken away;
ran away;
gave away;
walked away;
flying away.

These action words are listed on a chart.

Hints may be required to generate members for this list.
For example:
What could happen when you hold too many rocks in one hand?
What did the generous lady do when she had too many cookies?
What happened on a windy day to the apples on a tree?

Invite the child to,
  - *Think about events from around the home or the playground and use one of the words from the list to make up a story.*
  - *Show what happens in your story with counters.*

Accommodating Responses

Be attentive to the comments some children make, since the additive action can be part of the stories that are told for the subtractive action.

For example:
The generous lady *'gives away'*, but the recipient *'gets'*,
    or *'gets more.'*
Apples *'fall off'* the tree, but there will be *'more'* on the ground.

Some children need to be reminded to tell a story that talks about the *action,* since they may get off on a creative journey that begins with, *'Once upon a time ...'* and may not return to anything that is relevant at this point in time.

Summary Writing

Possible Materials:

- Counters
or toy animals and
sketches showing the
subtractive action:
- one of four balls rolling
off a table
- two of five birds leaving
a branch.

Present the sketch that shows the ball rolling off the table
and invite the child to,

- *Look at the balls.*
- *How many balls were sitting on the table before
one rolled off the table?*
- *Show with your fingers.*

- *What is happening to one of the balls?*
- *Show what is happening with your fingers.*

- *Talk about what is happening and tell the whole story
about the balls.*

Tell the child, we *print a summary for the story using number names
and the word* **minus**; *5 minus 1 where* **minus** *means* **take away**
or any other word that means separating or moving away.

Invite the child to:

- *Use number names and minus to tell about the sketch
with the birds.*
- *Print a summary for your story.*

- *Think about cats, dogs, cows or horses.*
- *Make up a story.*
- *Show what happens in your story with counters,
or with toy animals.*
- *Print a summary with number names and minus.*

Retell stories from the previous task *'Away' Stories* and record
summaries for these stories.

Explain the meanings of each part of the summaries as the action
of the stories is shown with counters.

Which Summary?

Possible Materials:

- Sketches showing the *subtractive action*:
  - a hand picking three of seven daisies standing in a row.
  - a hand picking two of five tulips standing in a row.

- Cards showing the summaries:
  - [4 – 3]
  - [7 – 3]
  - [3 – 2]
  - [5 – 2]

Present the sketch with the daisies to the child.
- *Show with counters how many daisies there are in the picture.*
- *Now show what you think is happening. Explain your thinking.*

Tell the child, *we can print **7 minus 3** as a summary for what is happening, or we can print **7 – 3**.*

*We read the sign [-] as **minus** and it can mean any of the words that talk about **taking away** or **separating**.*

- *Look at the picture with the tulips.*
- *Tell a story about what is happening.*

- *Which of these two summaries do you think tells what is happening in the picture?*   [5 – 2]   [3 – 2]

- *Why did you pick that one and not the other one?*
- *How do you know that is the correct choice?*
- *What does the first number name in a summary tells us?*
- *What does the second number name tell us?*

- *What story would you make up for the other summary?*

Present the same questioning sequence for the daisies and the choices:
[4 – 3]   [7 – 3]

'Away' Sketches

Materials:

- Sketch showing three of eight apples dropping off a branch.

- Sketches of a rectangular region.

Show a diagram of a rectangular region and a sketch of the apples. Invite the child to,
- *Tell an action story about the apples.*

Retell the story and model the *action* of the story by placing eight counters into the rectangular region and moving three counters out of the region.

Illustrate the story and the action in a pictorial way by drawing eight dots in a rectangular region, a loop around three of the dots and an arrow to the loop to indicate the *subtractive action*.

A summary for the story and diagram is recorded: **8 – 3**.

To prepare sketches for the subtractive action, ask the child to use the sketches of the rectangular regions, ovals with arrows and dots to show what happened for some of the summaries and stories from the previous tasks.

Further Tasks

Understanding Subtraction:

- For a given action diagram, i.e., rectangular region showing six counters; an oval with an arrow around two of these counters, ask the child to print a summary and make up a story for it.

- Give two summary choices for an action diagram, i.e., [4 – 2] and [6 – 2] for six apples on a table and two falling off. Ask the child to select the summary that belongs with the sketch and to make up an action story. Invite the child to draw an action diagram for the other summary and make up a story for it.

- Present two action diagrams and one summary, i.e., three objects with one moving away; four objects with one moving away; and [4 – 1]. After the child selects the diagram that belongs to the summary and makes up an appropriate action story for it, a summary and story are requested for the other action diagram.

Record Sheet Suggestions

How do children relate the **additive action** to events from their experiences?
How do children interpret the *additive action* presented to them as:

- simulations;
- action diagrams;
- summaries?

1. Examples of terms and phrases used to describe the *additive* action – ***'More' Stories***.

   _____

   _____

2. Example of a story for a summary, i.e., **5 + 3** that demonstrates an understanding of:
   - the *numbers*;
   - the *order* of the numbers, how many to begin with; how many were added;
   - the *additive* action – ***Summary Writing***.

   _____

   _____

3. Example of a story for a diagram that demonstrates an understanding of the *numbers*;
   the *order* of the numbers, how many to begin with; how many were added; and the *additive* action
   – ***Matching Sketches and Summaries***.

   _____

   _____

4. Explanations that include simulations with counters and action stories and show an understanding
   of the difference between examples like **2 + 4** and **4 + 2** – ***Matching Sketches and Summaries***.

   _____

   _____

5. Indicators of *confidence* and *willingness to take risks*. _____

   _____

Record Sheet Suggestions

How do children relate the **subtractive action** to events from their experiences?
How do children interpret the *subtractive action* presented to them as:
- simulations;
- action diagrams;
- summaries?

1. Examples of terms and phrases used to describe the *subtractive* action – **'Away' Stories**.

   _____

   _____

2. Example of a story for a *summary*, i.e., **6 - 4** that demonstrates an understanding of:
   - the *numbers*;
   - the *order* of the numbers,
   - the *subtractive* action – **Summary Writing**.

   _____

   _____

3. Example of a story for a diagram that demonstrates an understanding of the *numbers*;
   and the *subtractive* action.
   For example: rectangular region showing 6 counters; 2 of the counters enclosed in a loop
   with an arrow that indicates removal.
   Response to the question, *Why does the diagram not show the action for 4 - 2?*
   Which Summary?

   _____

   _____

4. Reaction to, *Tell me something about a summary like* **3 - 5**.

   _____

   _____

5. Indicators of *confidence* and *willingness to take risks*. _____

   _____

Basic Facts

What are the basic facts?

In most parts of the world *basic addition facts* include all possible single-digit (0 to 9) combinations. That means that there are one hundred *basic addition facts* ranging from,

0 + 0 = [ ] to **9 + 9 = [ ]**.

The *basic subtraction facts* can be thought of as the inverse of the basic addition facts. There are one hundred *basic subtraction facts*:
- the first number, or the minuend, is less than or equal to 18;
- the number that is taken away, or the subtrahend, is less than or equal to 9;
- the answer, or difference, is less than or equal to 9.

General Goals for Basic Facts

Children will be able to:
- use *mental mathematics strategies* so that they can teach the basic facts to themselves.
- use *mental mathematics strategies* to show, in more than one way, that the answers they give are correct.
- use *mental mathematics strategies* to reinvent facts that are forgotten.
- get unstuck when faced with not knowing the solution and to do so with a minimum of counting.
- be confident about their knowledge of the *basic facts* and commit as many as possible to memory.

Equality

Key Ideas and Questions

Before *summaries* are recorded as *equations*, aspects of the *equality relation* need to be introduced.

Children need to know that an *equation* is a mathematical sentence written with the symbol =, which is read as *'is equal to'* or *'is the same as.'*

The symbol does not mean, *'the answer is'*, *'makes'* or *'produces'*, but rather expresses an *equivalent relationship*. Instead of interpreting **4 + 3 = 7** as, *four plus three makes seven; four and three is equal to seven* relates **4** and **3** and **7** and vise versa.

Equations are *true* or *false*. This implies that many different responses for equations like **4 + 3 = [ ]** or **6 = 2 + [ ]** are possible. The box for these types of *equations* can be thought of as a number sorter. Only one number maintains equality and results in an *equation* that is *true*.

Is Equal To

Possible Materials:

- Five fingers or a sketch of five fingers.

- Cards showing:
  4 + [ ]
  2 + [ ] = 5
  4 = [ ] + [ ]

Point to the five fingers, or hold up five fingers.
The **4 + [ ]** is shown and ask the child,
- *What number would you have to add to 4 to get 5?*

After the answer is given, the child is told,
- *Five is equal to four plus one and we print:*
  5 is equal to or **the same as 4 + 1**
- *Rather than printing the words, we use this [=] sign and read it as, is equal to and we print:* **5 = 4 + 1**
- *A summary with an equal sign is called an equation.*

Look at **2 + [ ] = 5**
- *Which number makes this equation true? How do you know?*
- *How many fingers would you have to add to two fingers that would equal five fingers?*

Look at **4 = [ ] + [ ]**
- *Try to think of as many numbers as you can that makes the equation true.*

Basic Addition Facts

There are one hundred *basic addition facts*. The task of memorizing these facts can be quite a challenge and a very boring chore, especially for children who do not have a *sense of number* and are not developing *number sense*. The importance of *number sense* is illustrated by specific goals that are identified and the key activities that are described.

Specific Goals for the Basic Addition Facts

Children will be able to:

- use aspects of *number sense*: *recognition, flexible thinking,* and *visualization skills* to solve *equations* with answers of ten or less.
- generate rules for *addition fact equations* involving *zero* and *one* and test these rules.
- use *flexible thinking* about numbers that allows for the *going first to ten and then beyond* strategy for solving equations.
- use *flexible thinking* about numbers to develop a strategy for solving equations involving *doubles*.
- recognize equations with addends that are *almost doubles* and apply the knowledge about *doubles* to solve equations.
- recognize equations that have *addends that differ by two* and use *flexible thinking* about numbers and number names to change these addends to *doubles* in order to solve equations.

Possible Materials:

- Six fingers
or a sketch of six fingers
being held up – five on one hand
and one on the other.

- Cards showing:
  5 + 1 = 6
  6 = 5 + 1
  1 + 5 = 6
  6 = 1 + 5.

- Displays of fingers
or sketches of finger
arrangements showing:
- seven fingers, five fingers
  and two fingers;
- eight fingers, five fingers
  and three fingers;
- nine fingers, five fingers
  and four fingers;
  - ten fingers.

One of the activities for *cardinal number*, **Finger Flash**, deals with *recognition* of the number shown for different arrangements of fingers without having to count, a component of *number sense*.

Show the child six fingers and request,

- *Say something about the number six, or the parts that show six.*

- *Use your fingers to show the action for five plus one (5 + 1) by moving the one finger toward the five fingers.*

- *We can say, six is equal to five plus one, or five plus one is equal to six, and we can print these equations:*
  6 = 5 + 1   5 + 1 = 6

- *Show with your fingers what you think the action for one plus five is equal to six (1 + 5 = 6) would look like.*

- *Make up two stories,*
  - *one for five plus one is equal to six (5 + 1 = 6), and*
  - *one for one plus five is equal to six (1 + 5 = 6).*

- *How are the stories different?*
- *What is the same about the stories?*

Repeat the above key questions, simulations and recordings for the arrangements showing **seven**, **eight**, **nine** and **ten** fingers.

Other Names

Possible Materials:

- Arrangements of fingers or sketches of six fingers, five on one hand, one on the other.

- Seven and eight fingers are shown with five and two, and five and three fingers, respectively.

Flexible thinking about numbers is an important part of number sense.

Present each arrangement of fingers and invite the child to,
- *Look at the fingers on one hand.*
- *Tell how many fingers there are.*
- *Use the fingers on both hands to show the number in a different way.*
- *Now use your way of showing the number to tell and act out a story that involves the addition action.*
- *Tell what equation can be printed for your story and the action.*

Accommodating Responses

It may be necessary to illustrate the intent with an example.

If two and three are shown for the request to show five fingers in a different way, move the three fingers toward the two fingers and record two equations: **5 = 2 + 3   2 + 3 = 5**

- *What story can you tell and what equation can you print for the action that has the three fingers moving toward the two fingers?*

- *What is another way of showing five with the fingers of two hands?* (**4 and 1**; **5 and 0**)

- *Tell different stories and show the actions for adding. Print the equations for these stories and actions?*

Make similar requests as the child thinks of different finger arrangements for the numbers six, seven, and eight and simulates the additive action in different ways.

As the child deals with each number ask,
- *How do you know you have thought about all the possible combinations of fingers to show this number?*

More to Five or Ten

Possible Materials:

- Arrangements of fingers or sketches of:
  three fingers on one hand;
  seven fingers, five and two.

Visualization skills are involved when we ask children to tell how many fingers they see and then how many they think they cannot see, or how many more fingers are needed to show either five fingers or ten fingers.

Show three fingers and ask,
- *How many fingers do you see?*
- *How many fingers on this hand do you think you do not see?*
- *How do you know?*

- *How many fingers have to be added to the three fingers to show five fingers?*
- *What equation can be printed for adding two fingers to show five fingers?*   **3 + 2 = 5**

Repeat the sequence of questions for the numbers **one**, **two**, **four** and **five**.

Show seven fingers and ask,
- *How many fingers do you see?*
- *How many fingers do you think are not shown? How do you know?*
- *How many fingers have to be added to show all ten fingers?*
- *What equation can be printed for adding three fingers to show ten fingers?*   **7 + 3 = 10**

Repeat the questions,
- *How many fingers do you see?*
- *How many fingers cannot be seen?*
for showing **six**, **eight**, **nine** and **ten** fingers.

Print matching equations.

These activities and questions indicate that the major components of *number sense*: recognition, *flexible thinking* and *visualization skills* allow for easy transfer to *addition equations*. More than one-half of the one hundred *basic addition facts* are solved without senseless repetition, boring practice or meaningless speed tests.

One and Zero

Materials:

- Piece of paper showing four items:

    3 + 1 = [ ]
    7 + 1 = [ ]
    5 + 1 = [ ]
    8 + 1 = [ ]

- Several equations with zero as an addend:

    4 + 0 = [ ]
    0 + 6 = [ ]
    0 + 8 = [ ]
    9 + 0 = [ ]

As part of *mathematical thinking* the child is asked to make and test *generalizations*.

Present the equations with one as an addend.
Invite the child to,
- *Print the answers.*

Look at these equations.
- *What is the same about them?*
- *Why do you think finding the answer for these is easy?*

- *If you were to make up your own rule for finding the answer when one is added to a number, what would the rule be?*

- *Do you think your rule would always work?*
- *Try it with a big number and explain what happens.*

The intent of the questions is for the child to relate adding one to counting.

If that goal is reached, the child could be asked to compare this to equations that have one as the first addend: **1 + 6 = [ ]   1 + 4 = [ ]**
- *What is different?*
- *Is there anything the same?*

Invite a response to the following,
- *Do you think it is possible to think of the biggest number that exists? Why or why not?*

Present the equations with zero as an addend.
The requests for responses include,
- *Print the answers.*
- *What is the same about these equations?*
- *What would your rule be for finding the answers when zero is added to a number or a number is added to zero?*
- *Do you think your rule will always work? Why or why not?*
- *Try it with a big number and explain what happens.*

Doubles

Material:

- Piece of paper showing:
    - 6 + 6 = [ ]
    - 7 + 7 = [ ]
    - 8 + 8 = [ ]
    - 9 + 9 = [ ]

Present a partial list of doubles to the child.

3 + 3 = [ ]   5 + 5 = [ ]   6 + 6 = [ ]   8 + 8 = [ ]   .

Invite the child to,
- *Print a few others that you think could belong to this list of equations.*
- *How did you know what to print?*
- *How are all of these equations in some way the same?*

Tell the child, *we call these equations **doubles**.*
- *Why do you think that name is used for these equations?*

For **6 + 6 = [ ]**, show a six to the child with five fingers on one hand and one on the other. The child is asked to show a six in the same way. Place both sixes on the table.
- *Look at the fingers showing the two sixes on the table.*
- *Try to think of a way that would make it very easy for us to tell how many fingers there are?*
- *How could we tell how many there are without having to count every finger?*

The intent is to connect this task to what was done to make sense of the *teen numbers* and *numerals*.

If we move the two hands that show fives together, we are looking at one ten and two more, or twelve. We print the equation **6 + 6 = 12**.

Use the same strategy to write equations for other doubles.

The problem of not always having a friend available to show one of the doubles is discussed.
- *Try to think of a way to figure out the answer by just looking at your fingers.*

Accommodating Responses

Some children need guiding questions to pretend to have two fives, count these twice and then add two groups of the remaining fingers.

Almost Doubles

Materials:

- Piece of paper showing:
  - 6 + 7 = [ ]
  - 8 + 7 = [ ]
  - 6 + 5 = [ ]
  - 8 + 9 = [ ]

Accommodating Responses

Ask the child to look at the piece of paper.
- *Try to think of something that is the same for all of these equations.*

- *If you think you have found something that is the same, try to print a few more equations that you think belong to this list.*
- *Explain your thinking.*

Some guiding questions may be required to have the child reach the conclusion that, *one of the number names is one more.*

Once a conclusion like, *'There is a gap of one between the two number names'* is reached, ask the child,
- *Why do you think these are called **near doubles** or **almost doubles**?*

Invite the child to,
- *Look at (**6 + 7 = [ ]** is pointed to) and think of a double that is close to the number names in this equation.*
- *What double are you thinking of?*

- *How does knowing the answer for that double help you find the answer for the equation?*
- *If you use the answer for six plus six and your rule for adding one to a number, what will the answer be?*

- *Use the same way to figure out the answers for the other equations with number names that are almost doubles.*
- *Explain what you are thinking.*

A Gap of Two

Materials:

- Counters.

- A piece of paper showing:
  - 4 + 6 = [ ]
  - 7 + 5 = [ ]
  - 1 + 3 = [ ]
  - 6 + 8 = [ ]

Accommodating Responses

Ask the child to look at the piece of paper with the equations,
- *Try to think of something that is the same for all of these equations.*
- *If you think you have found something that is the same, print a few more equations that you think can belong to this list.*

Give the child at least the opportunity to have two tries to discover the intended similarities, before presenting guiding questions that enable the realization that the addends differ by two.

Once this stage is reached invite the child to,
- *Print a few more equations that belong to this list.*
- *If you make up a name for equations like these, what would you call them? Why?*

Ask the child to think about the question until it is returned to after a few more activities.

One equation is selected, i.e., **4 + 6 = [ ]**.
Ask the child to,
- *Show the four and the six with two rows of counters and place one row above other.*
- *What do you think we could do to find out how many counters there are?*

Demonstrate the *share ono to make a double* strategy, that is taking one counter from the row of six and moving it to the row of four counters.

The new equation now is **5 + 5 = [ ]**, a familiar double.

Make the requests,
- *Below each of the equations record the double these equations could be changed to.*
- *Record the answers.*
- *Choose two equations and use counters to explain and show how the answer can be found.*

Search and Tell

Materials:

- A sheet of paper with a list of twenty or more *basic addition facts* equations. The list includes four *doubles*, four *almost doubles* and four examples with a *gap of two* between the number names.

- Three different coloured pencils.

Before the *mental mathematics strategies* that have been learned can be applied, the child needs to be able to find examples for these strategies.

Present the list and invite the child to,
- *Use different colours to identify each of the following:*
  - *Use red to underline any equations that are doubles..*
  - *Use blue to underline any equations that are almost doubles..*
  - *Use green to underline any equations that have a gap of two between the two number names to be added.*

- *Explain and show a way or strategy, other than counting, for finding the answers for each type.*

- *Print the answers.*

First to Ten

Materials:

- A piece of paper showing:
  7 + 5 = [ ]
  8 + 6 = [ ]
  9 + 5 = [ ]
  6 + 7 = [ ]

- Arrangements of fingers or sketches of fingers.

Display several arrangements of fingers, one at a time.
For each group of fingers that is displayed, ask the child,
- *Tell and show how many more are needed to show all ten of the fingers?*

Ask the child to,
- *Use the fingers on both hands to show and name five in three different ways.* **3 and 2; 4 and 1; 5 and 0**

The equation **7 + 5 = [ ]** is presented. Ask the child,
- *If you were to find the answer for this equation, which way of showing and naming five would to you use to go to ten?*
- *What would you have to add to ten to get the answer?*

As each equation is presented in turn, invite the child to,
- *State the number names for six (five and seven) that would make it possible to go to ten first, and then beyond to get the answer.*

More Search and Tell

Materials:

- Prepare a list similar to the one for the *Search and Tell* activity.

- Include a fourth category and colour.

Ask the child to underline and solve equations for the *First to Ten* strategy.

Two or More Ways

Materials:

- Piece of paper showing the equations:
  8 + 6 = [ ]
  9 + 7 = [ ]
  8 + 6 = [ ]
  is presented.

Request the child to,
- *Try and think of as many different ways as you can, other than counting by ones, for finding the answer.*
- *Try to write equations that show your thinking for each of the ways you have thought of.*

The same requests are made for the equation **9 + 7 = [ ]**.

**Practice
and
Confidence**

We want children to beam with confidence when they demonstrate that they know the *basic addition facts* and know at least two ways, other than counting, to convince someone that the answers they know are correct. They should be able to explain the *strategies* they can or could use to reinvent an answer should it be forgotten. How do children get to this stage of *numerical flexibility* and *power*? What role does *practice* play?

Practice is necessary for learning mathematics. However, some forms of practice are *appropriate*, while other forms are inappropriate. *Appropriate meaningful* settings provide opportunities for *reasoning, communicating, connecting, expressing, representing,* and furthering the development of *number sense.* These are also settings that children want to participate in. Good games meet some of the criteria of *appropriate practice* and we include a couple of examples in the last chapter. We do not consider speed tests and taking practice sheets with simple instructions like *add* or *solve* or *find the answer* taken from the internet or from other references appropriate practice settings.

Some educators believe that *rote learning* is an *oxymoron*. There are those who believe that timed tests do not contribute to mathematics learning. There are those who believe that rote or inappropriate practice will not contribute in any way to the development of *conceptual understanding* and *number sense*. We agree with these educators and the many children we have interviewed and tried to help convinced us that these educators are right.

Record Sheet Suggestions

The key questions are:
- What *mental mathematics strategies* does the child use to check an answer and to explain that an answer is correct?
- What *strategies* does the child use, other than counting, to get unstuck if an answer is forgotten or unknown?

1. Rules made up for finding the answers when one is added to a number and when zero is added to a number. Examples used to test these rules – **One and Zero**.

   _____

   _____

2. Number of responses given for each example in the format: **a = [ ] + [ ]**.
   For example, **8 = [ ] + [ ]**; **13 = [ ] + [ ]** and the answers to the question,
   *What number names do you think could be hidden behind the boxes? – **Is Equal To**.*

   _____

   _____

3. Responses to, *What are several different things you can do and say to convince another child that the following equations are true? – **A Gap of Two**.*
   $$8 + 6 = 14 \qquad 7 + 9 = 16$$

   _____

   _____

4. Responses to, *Pretend you forgot an answer. Explain your thinking for the different things you could do to figure out the answer? – **First to Ten; A Gap of Two**.*
   $$5 + 8 = [ ] \qquad 9 + 6 = [ ] \qquad 7 + 9 = [ ]$$

   _____

   _____

5. Responses to, *If you were to use your fingers to show and to explain to someone how to find the answer for **7 + 6 = [ ]**, how would you do it? What would you say? – **Almost Doubles**; **First to Ten**.*

   _____

   _____

6. Responses to, *If there is one answer for an addition equation that you seem to forget or that seems a little more difficult, what do you do to try to remember it or to figure it out?*

   _____

   _____

7. Indicators of *confidence* and *willingness to take risks*. _____

   _____

Basic Subtraction Facts

Some references that are used in our schools introduce *basic addition* and *subtraction facts* at the same time.
For example:

$$3 + 2 = 5 \qquad 5 - 2 = 3 \qquad 5 - 3 = 2$$

This can be confusing for children.

There are one hundred *basic subtraction facts*, $a - b = c$, where **a** is **18** or less, **b** is **9** or less, and **c** is **9** or less.

We want to show children that learning these basic facts is not difficult if they use what they know about numbers and the *basic addition facts*.

The importance of *number sense* and knowledge of the *basic addition facts* is illustrated in the described activities.

Specific Goals for the Basic Subtraction Facts

Children will be able to:
* generate rules for subtracting *zero* and *one* from a number and *subtracting a number from itself* and test these rules.
* explain how the answer for every *basic subtraction fact* equation can be obtained from a known *basic addition fact*.

Match the Action

Possible Materials:

- Arrangements of fingers, or sketches of fingers, showing seven in two different ways: five and two; four and three.

  - Cards showing:

    7 – 2 = [ ]
    7 – 5 = [ ]
    7 – 4 = [ ]
    7 – 3 = [ ]

Invite the child to,

- *Use your fingers to show the action and the answer for five plus two.*
- *How can you use your fingers to show the action and the answer for seven take away two?*
- *What is the answer?*
- *Print your answer on the card.* **7 – 2 = [ ]**

- *Show five plus two again. Now show the action and the answer for seven take away five.*
- *What is the answer?*
- *Print the answer on the card.* **7 – 5 = [ ]**

- *Use fingers to show the action and the answer for four plus three.*
- *Now show the action and the answer for seven take away four.*
- *Print the answer on the card.* **7 – 4 = [ ]**

- *Show the action and answer for seven take away three.*
- *Print the answer on the card.* **7 – 3 = [ ]**

Matching Equations

Materials:

- Cards with a representative sample of *basic addition equations* with an answer of ten or less.

  - For example:

    5 + 3 = [ ]
    6 + 4 = [ ]
    7 + 2 = [ ]
    3 + 6 = [ ]

Present the cards, one at a time, and ask the child to print the answer. For example: **5 + 3 = [ ]**

Invite the child to,

- *Try and print the subtraction equations and the answers that you think go with the addition equation.*
- *Use your fingers or counters to show that your answers are correct.*
- *Explain what you are doing.*

How Do You Know?

Materials:

- Cards with a representative sample of *basic subtraction facts* with minuends greater than ten.

  For example:
  - 13 – 6 = [ ]
  - 15 – 8 = [ ]
  - 16 – 9 = [ ]
  - 17 – 8 = [ ]
  - 12 – 5 = [ ]
  - 14 – 7 = [ ]
  - 11 – 6 = [ ]

Show a card to the child.
For example: **13 – 6 = [ ]**
Make comments like the following:
- *I know that two is not the correct answer, because two plus six is not equal to thirteen.*
- *I know that three is not the correct answer, because three plus six is not thirteen.*
- *How do you know that four, five and six are not the correct answers?*
- *How do you know seven is the correct answer?*

15 – 8 = [ ] is presented for examination.
- *Tell me some numbers that are not the correct answers and why you know that they are not the correct answers.*
- *Tell me the number that is the correct answer.*
- *How do you know it is the correct number?*

For each example invite the child to,
- *Print the answer and tell how you know that the answer is correct.*

The child is told,
- *Look at the examples and identify the equations that you think are not true.*
- *How do you know the answer is incorrect?*
- *How do you know the other answers are correct?*

18 – 9 = 10	11 – 9 = 2	15 – 6 = 11	12 – 8 = 5
13 – 8 = 5	14 – 6 = 6	17 – 8 = 10	

Test Your Rule

Materials:

- Three sets of three cards with subtraction equations.

  Each set contains similar items.
  The first card in each set shows
  4 – 4 = [ ];
  5 – 1 = [ ];
  and
  3 – 0 = [ ],
  respectively.

The procedure for each set of cards is the same.
- *What is the same about these equations?*
- *Print the answers.*
- *Why is finding the answers for these equations easy?*
- *If you were to make up your own rule for finding the answers when a number is subtracted from itself, (when one is subtracted from a number; when zero is subtracted from a number) what would it be?*
- *Do you think your rule would always work? Why or why not?*
- *Test your rule with a big number.*

Record Sheet Suggestions

The main aspects of *mathematical thinking* that are part of this data collection include information about how a child *generalizes* and *applies* such generalizations, and how a child *connects* the *basic subtraction facts* to knowledge of *basic addition facts*.

1. Rules made up for finding the answers for:
    a – a = [ ]   a – 0 = [ ]   a – 1 = [ ].
    Examples used to test these rules. – *Test Your Rule.*

    _____

    _____

2. Responses to, *What is the answer and how do you know the answer is correct?*
    For examples like **9 – 4 = [ ]** and **16 – 9 = [ ]** – *How Do You Know?*

    _____

    _____

3. Responses to, *Pretend you forgot an answer.*
    Explain your thinking for the different things you could do to figure out the answer:
    17 – 9 = [ ]   13 – 8 = [ ]   12 – 7 = [ ] – *Matching Equations* and *How Do You Know?*

    _____

    _____

4. Responses to,
    If you were to use your fingers to show someone how to find the answer for **14 – 6 = [ ]**,
    how would you do it?
    What would you say?
    Try to think of two different ways.

    _____

    _____

    _____

5. Indicators of *confidence* and *willingness to take risks.* _____

    _____

Spatial Sense

Spatial sense, an integral part of numeracy, includes spatial reasoning and visual imagery. Spatial sense is a necessary part of problem solving and therefore, of children's success in mathematics.

Spatial sense is important to other aspects of learning. These include such things as writing letters and numerals; interpreting and preparing tables; making and reading plans and maps; following directions; and building models.

Just like number sense, spatial abilities can be developed. It is possible to create activity settings and orchestrate discussions that foster the development and improvement of spatial sense.

The suggestions for the activities focus on engaging children in examining aspects of three-dimensional figures. These activities and settings, as well as introductory activities for two-dimensional figures, are presented with the intent to develop children's spatial sense.

Three-Dimensional Figures

The emphasis will be on activities with three-dimensional figures. Most obvious is the fact that we live in a three-dimensional world. From now on, we refer to three-dimensional figures as blocks. Blocks are easily manipulated and they allow for an easy transition to the exploration of two-dimensional figures.

Since the focus of these activity settings is on having children consider the geometric attributes of blocks as well as the similarities and differences between blocks, it makes sense for the set of blocks to be colourless, or for all blocks to be of the same colour. It is also advantageous for a set of blocks to include duplicates, as well as blocks that are similar in shape.

It is important to note that the development of spatial sense does not require the child to memorize or recall the names of blocks that have a special shape. Most children are familiar with some names, but many of these names are used incorrectly. Some children may want to know the names of blocks like: cube, sphere, cylinder, cone, pyramid, and prism and there is no harm in applying these names correctly; however, there are no advantages in doing so.

(continued next page ...)

Spatial Sense (cont'd)

**Specific Goals
for
Three-Dimensional
Figures**

The goals indicate that the focus of the activities is on attempting to foster the development of *visualization skills*. As can be seen, the strategies of *sorting*, *matching* and *ordering* play an important role in this development.

Children will be able to:
- connect blocks to objects in their environment and conclude, *what a block reminds me of depends on the direction from where I look at it.*
- look at a given block and explain responses to selecting or pointing to a block that is: exactly like it; a little bit like it; like it, but smaller; like it, but bigger; completely different.
- look at photographs or diagrams of blocks and match them to blocks and hold them in the same position.
- identify information required to create a copy of a building given its front view.
- explain how all *faces* on blocks are the same and how they can differ.
- classify blocks according to number of *faces* or *characteristics* of *faces*.
- look at blocks from a distance, identify how many *faces* can be seen and make a prediction about how many cannot be seen. Check the prediction and suggest other possible answers.
- match tracings of the different *faces* of a block with a block that matches these *faces* and tell how many faces of each type the block has.
- assume that a drawing of one *face* is a view of a block and try to match it with an appropriate block or with appropriate blocks; explain the reason(s) for the selection(s).
- explain how *edges* on blocks differ and classify blocks according to number of edges or characteristics of *edges*.
- identify *corners* on blocks and use *faces*, *edges* and *corners* for sorting tasks.
- examine a block placed out of view behind the back and explain how the examining of *faces*, *edges* or *corners* is helpful in identifying from a collection of blocks a block that is: *exactly like it; a little like it; like it, but smaller; like it, but bigger; completely different.*
- look at photographs or diagrams, tell how many *faces*, *edges* and *corners* are seen and make predictions about how many *faces*, *edges* and *corners* are not seen. Find a block to check each prediction. Explain why different answers might be possible.
- use *faces*, *edges* and *corners* to create a difference train where the next car (block) differs in at least one way; in at least two ways.
- look at four blocks and use *faces*, *edges* and *corners* to provide two or more answers to, *Which block do you think does not belong? Why?*

What Does it Look Like?

Materials:

- A collection of blocks
  that are colourless
  or
  the same colour.

Ask the child to select one block and respond to these types of questions,
- *What does this block remind you of?*
- *Turn the block a little, what does it remind you of now?*
- *Turn the block a little more, what does it remind you of now?*
- *Put the block on the floor, stand right above it and look down at it.
  What does it remind you of now?*
- *Take the block and hold it above your head.
  What does it remind you of now?*
- *Why is it that one block can remind us of different things?*

Select a different block and pose similar questions.

Selecting

Materials:

- A collection of blocks
  of the same colour
  or
  colourless.

- One block beside the box.

These tasks invite children to use their language to describe comparisons among blocks.

Prompt the child to,
- *Look at the block beside the box. Try to find a block from
  the box that is exactly like the block.*
- *How would you say the blocks are the same?*
- *Is there anything else that is the same about the two blocks?*

- *Find and pick out a block from the box that is like the one
  beside the box, but is smaller.*
- *What do you think is the same about the two blocks?*

Repeat the task and make similar requests for a block that is,
like it but is bigger.

Challenge the child to,
- *Pick out a block from the box that you think is very different
  from the block beside the box. In what ways do you think
  the two blocks are different?*

Repeat the procedure, or a variation thereof, by placing a different block beside the box.

Try to Match It

Materials:

- A collection of blocks.

- Small pieces of paper with sketches or photographs of different blocks.

- Several sketches or photographs that show the same block from different view-points.

Tell the child that each of the sketches is a drawing of one of the blocks in the box.

The child is challenged to,
- *Try to find the block that is shown and try to hold it in the same way as in the picture.*
- *What does the block remind you of when you hold it like that?*

Present the sketches or digital photographs that show the same block from different view-points and invite the child to,
- *Try to find the block that you think is shown and try to hold it like it is shown in the drawings.*
- *Explain what you are thinking.*
- *If the different positions remind you of different things, tell what these are.*

Buildings – Same and Different

Materials:

- A collection of blocks.

- A sketch of a frontal view of a building made of six blocks.

- A sketch of a top view of a building.

Ask the child to look at the sketch of the frontal view of the building.
- *Show on your fingers how many blocks you think were used for the building.*
- *What do you think you would have to do to find out the exact number of blocks that are part of the building?*

- *Pretend that there are no blocks hidden or behind the building.*
- *Try to build one that is exactly like it.*
- *Explain what you are thinking as you are choosing your blocks and as you are building.*

Ask the child to explain the thinking that is done as the child selects blocks for the following challenges,
- *Look at the picture of the building and build one that is like it, but is smaller.*
- *Try to build one that is like it, but is bigger.*
- *Build one that is completely different. How is it different?*

It Reminds Me Of – and More

Materials:

- A collection of blocks.

While the child is not looking select a block and place it into the hands behind the back.

- *Without looking at the block and only feeling all around it, tell what you think the block reminds you of.*

- *Turn the block slowly in your hands.*
- *If it reminds you of something different as you turn it, what is it?*

- *Now show the block and explain what you were thinking as you felt the block..*

Repeat the task with different blocks.

All About Faces

Materials:

- A set of several different blocks, including some with round faces.

Select a block. Tell the child, *the big part of a block is called a **face***.

- *As you take different blocks into your hands, show and feel the faces of these blocks.*
- *Look at the blocks.*
- *Try to think of something that is the same for all of the faces on the blocks.*

Accommodating Responses

Hints may be necessary to have the child conclude that they all are *smooth*.

- *How can faces on different blocks be different?*

Choose blocks and provide hints to enable the child to conclude that faces can be *round, flat, big* and *small* and that they can have *different shapes*.

After the child selects a block, invite the child to,

- *Tell how many faces the block has.*
- *Why is it not so easy to count the faces on a block that has many faces?*
- *What do you think could be done to make the counting of faces and keeping track of faces easy or easier when they are counted?*

Face Count

Materials:

- Seven pieces of paper labelled:
  1 face;
  2 faces;
  3 faces;
  4 faces;
  5 faces;
  6 faces;
  More than 6 faces,
  respectively.

- A collection of many different blocks.

Accommodating Responses

Place the pieces of paper onto a table or on the floor and make the request,

- *Pick up a block, count the faces and place the block onto the appropriate piece of paper.*
- *Repeat this with the other blocks and put these where they belong.*

After counting and sorting, pose the *open-ended* question,

- *Do you notice anything about the blocks on the different pieces of paper?*

More specifically, ask the child to respond to,

- *Which piece of paper or group has the most blocks?*
- *Which piece of paper or group has the fewest blocks?*

If the collection of blocks includes blocks of the same *shape* but different *sizes*, the child's answer to the following question enables an interesting discovery; that is, blocks that look different are in some way the same:

- *Look at the blocks that have six faces.*
- *We know how these blocks are the same because they have the same number of faces, but how are they different?*

If one piece of paper does not have a block on it, ask the child,

- *Do you think it is possible to have a block with that many faces?*

If the answer is '*yes*', then let's try to find one; if the answer is '*no*',

- *Why do you think that is the case?*

Ask the child to respond to and provide a reason for the answer to,

- *Do you think it is possible to have a block with zero faces?*

See and Cannot See – Parts of Blocks

Materials:

• A collection of blocks.

Hold up one block some distance away from the child.

Invite the child to,
• *Use fingers on one hand and show how many faces you can see.*
• *Use the fingers on the other hand to show how many faces you think you cannot see.*

Count the faces on the block to ensure all faces are accounted for.

Hold the block in a different way.
As before, ask,
• *How many faces can you see?*
• *How many faces do you think you cannot see?*

If the answers differ from the previous response, ask the child,
• *Why do you think the answers are different from before?*

Accommodating Responses

If several children are part of the activity, ask each child to take up a different position.

Invite the children to look at the answers and explain,
• *Why do you think the answers for the two questions, are not the same for different children?*
• *How many faces can you see? and How many faces do you think you cannot see?*

Repeat the same task with a different block.

Care is necessary for responses that do not agree. Different possible scenarios exist for the answers to differ.

One child may visualize a block that is different from what the other children have in mind. It could be that a child does not visualize the hidden faces. It could also be that a simple counting error has been made.

Match With the Faces

Materials:

- Several pieces of paper. Each piece of paper shows the tracings of the different faces of a block.

- A collection of blocks that includes the blocks that were used for the tracings.

Accommodating Responses

Present one piece of paper.

Tell the child,
- *The tracings show the different kinds of faces of one of the blocks.*
- *Try to find the block that has these different faces.*
- *How can you show that it is the right block?*

The child may need to be reminded that the different types of faces of a block were traced. This means that an idea about matching a face of a block with the tracing can be tested by fitting the face of the block onto the tracing.

Even after a reminder, some children still try to arrive at a fit for two faces that do not match. It is amazing the twists and turns they employ as part of this attempt.

- *How many faces of each type does the block have?*
Record the answers inside the tracings.

- *How many faces does the block have?*
- *Show all of the different faces on the block.*

Prior to repeating the procedure with a different set of sketches of faces, invite the child to look at all of the blocks and respond to the request,
- *Just by quickly looking at all of the blocks and at the tracings of the faces, which block or which blocks do you think will not match with the drawings of these faces?*
- *Why do you think so?*

See and Cannot See – Drawings

Possible Materials:

- Sketches of three blocks from different view-points.

  For example:
  - A triangular prism with two visible faces.
  - A frontal side view from above a rectangular prism with three visible faces.
  - A direct frontal view of a block showing a square face.

  Beside each sketch of the blocks the headings:
- **Number of Faces I Can See**;
- **Number of Faces I think I Cannot See**.

For each sketch, ask the child,
- *How many faces can you see?*
- *Show with your fingers.*

Record the answer under the appropriate heading.

- *Show with your fingers how many faces you think you cannot see.*

Record the answer and invite the child to,
- *Try and find the block that you think matches the picture.*
- *Count the faces.*
- *Could that be the block that is shown, or do you think is it a different block?*
- *Explain your thinking.*

Repeat the procedure for the diagram of the rectangular prism.

Examine the diagram of the square face and ask the child,
- *How many faces can be seen?*
- *How many faces do you think cannot be seen?*
- *Try to find the block that you are thinking of.*

After the child selects a block, invite the child to look at all of the available blocks and ask,
- *Do you think other answers are possible?*
- *If so, what do you think they might be?*

Accommodating Responses

The goal is to show the child that other possibilities exist. We cannot tell what the block looks like unless we have another view of a block.

As was the case for **See and Cannot See – Parts of Blocks**, care is needed as different responses are dealt with. Possible reasons for different responses can go beyond a child visualizing a different block. The reasons include such thing as: lack of visualization; a counting error; and visualizing a unique block that is not 'regular' and is not part of the collection.

Edges

Materials:

• A collection of blocks.

Show and tell the child that an **edge** of a block is the part where two faces come together. Make the requests,
- *Pick up two blocks and with your finger trace some of the edges.*
- *What do you think is the same about all of the edges you have felt and traced?*
- *Look at the blocks, how can edges be different?*

- *Try to find a block with one edge.*
- *Try to find a block with two edges.*
- *Find·two blocks that you think have many edges?*
- *Try to find a block with zero edges.*

Create riddle settings for the child: *Which block could it be?* For example,
- *I am thinking of a block that has twelve edges and all of the faces have the same shape.*
- *Which block am I thinking of?*
- *Do you think more than one answer is possible? Why or why not?*

Corners and Difference Trains

Materials:

• A set of several different blocks, including some with round faces.

Show and tell the child that a **corner** of a block is the part where edges come together. Make the requests,
- *Look at the corners on the blocks. What is the same about them?*

Make the following requests,
- *Try and find a block without corners.*
- *Try to find one with one corner.*
- *Try to find a block with four corners and one with five corners.*
- *Which blocks have many corners?*

One Difference Train

Place one block in front of the child and explain,

> For building a **One Difference Train**, the next block or car has to be different in at least one way. Before the block you choose becomes part of the train, you have to explain how the block is different in one way. You can talk about **faces** or **edges** or **corners**.

Two Difference Train

The rules are the same as for the **One Difference Train**, but now two differences are identified for every new car that becomes part of the train. Differences have to be explained in terms of **faces** and/or **edges** and/or **corners**.

Some children might enjoy the challenge of trying to build a **Three Difference Train**.

Which Could Not Belong?

Materials:

- Four different blocks.

The child faces the four blocks and is invited to,

- *Look at faces, edges and corners and tell which of the four blocks you think is in some way different or does not belong?*
- *Explain how the block is different.*

After identifying one block as different, repeat the requests,

- *Which other block do you think is in some way different?*
- *How is it different from the other three blocks?*

Some children may be *flexible* in their thinking and make suggestions for how each of the blocks could be in some way different from the others.

After discussing the differences, ask the child,

- *Try to think of all of the ways you can to tell how these four blocks are in some way the same?*

Feel It and Try to Tell

Materials:

- A collection of different blocks that contains duplicates as well as similar blocks.

Repeat the task of placing a block into a child's hands behind the back, but this time ask the child to feel the block and to think about the **faces**, **edges** and **corners** and try to find a block that is:

- *exactly like it.*
- *like it, but smaller.*
- *like it, but bigger.*
- *a little bit like it.*
- *completely different.*

After each selection, ask the child to explain which part of the block helped to find the block that was asked for.

Repeat the task with different blocks.

Two-Dimensional Figures

Topological properties can be used to introduce children to *closed curves*, e.g., a simple rubber band, and *closed curves* with *special shapes*, e.g., a *rectangle*, or other *two-dimensional figures*.

It is also possible to use *blocks* to make the transition from *three-dimensional* to *two-dimensional figures*. The result of tracing a face of a block onto a piece of paper results in three distinct parts:
- the tracing;
- the area inside the tracing;
- the area outside the tracing.

Special shapes of tracings are assigned the names many children are familiar with:
- *triangle*;
- *rectangle* and *square* (the special rectangle);
- *circle*.

Specific Goals for Two-Dimensional Figures

Children will be able to:
- identify and name the parts of the special shapes of two-dimensional figures.
- state how all *triangles* are the same and how they differ.
- state how all *rectangles* are the same and how they differ.
- state how all *circles* are the same and how they differ.

Triangular Faces

Materials:

- A pyramid
on a piece of paper
aside a tracing of a *triangle*.

- A collection of blocks.

Show a drawing of a multi-sided figure to the child and point to the parts called *sides*.

Invite the child to look at the tracing of the triangle and make the request,
- *Show on your fingers how many sides there are.*
  Trace the three sides with your finger.
- *Show on your fingers how many corners there are.*
  Point to the corners.

Tell the child, *whenever a shape has three straight sides and three corners, we call it a* **triangle** and make the request,
- *Trace the triangle.*
- *Point to the inside of the triangle.*
- *Point to the outside of the triangle.*

Invite the child to look at the blocks.
- *Select the blocks that have a face that has the shape of a triangle.*

After selecting several blocks, trace different triangular faces on a piece of paper and invite the child to,
- *Look at all of the triangles and tell how you think triangles can be different.*

Request a child who is six or older to,,
- *Try and draw as many different looking triangles as you can.*
- *How are all of the different looking triangles you have drawn the same?*

If children younger than six years old are asked to draw triangles that look different, their 'scribbles' will indicate that at an early age only the characteristics of inside and outside for a simple closed curve can be translated onto paper. Young children may lack the ability to draw three straight sides that meet at the corners.

Models of Triangles

Possible Materials:

- Many pieces of
drinking straws
of different lengths
and
pieces of pipe cleaners;

Or,
- Sticks of different lengths
and Plasticine.

When children create triangles with models like sticks and balls of Plasticine, or with straws and pipe cleaners, the definition of *triangle,* the union of three segments, is illustrated.

Make the following request,
- *Use the pieces of drinking straws and pipe cleaners and try to make as many different looking triangles as you can think of.*

When the task is completed, ask the child,
- *How are all of the triangles the same?*
- *How can triangles be different?*

Pose the following problems,
- *Do you think it might be possible to move two or more triangles together to make different looking triangles? Try it.*
- *Explain what you are trying to do.*

- *Use the pipe cleaners and straws try to make something that you think is not a triangle. How is it different?*

Present the following scenarios,
- *If everything in your house was shaped like a triangle, what things would look unusual or funny to you? Why?*
- *Do you think there are some things in your house that would not work if they were shaped like a triangle?*

If the answer is *'yes'*,
- *What are they and why do you think that is that the case?*

- *Try to make a sketch of part of a room where everything is in the shape of a triangle*
- *Tell a story about this part of the room.*

Rectangular Faces

Materials:

- A rectangular prism on a piece of paper aside a tracing of a *rectangle*.

- A collection of blocks.

- Two pieces of paper.

Tell the child, *a shape with four sides and four corners like 'this'* (point to parts of the tracing of the rectangle) *is called a **rectangle**.*

Trace several rectangular faces from various blocks onto the same sheet.

Look at the rectangles.
- *What do you think is the same about all of the rectangles?*
- *How can rectangles look different?*

Present the two pieces of paper and make the request,
- *Sort the blocks into two groups, those that have rectangular faces and those that do not.*
- *Why is it possible for some blocks to belong to or be put on both sheets of paper?*

If, by chance, a young child does not believe that a **square** is a special **rectangle**, introduce a third piece of paper with a tracing of a square face for a three way sorting task.

Different Shapes of Faces

Materials:

- Three pieces of paper with tracings of a *triangle*, a *rectangle*, and a *circle*, respectively.

- A collection of blocks.

The child is invited to,
- *Look at the tracings of the faces and put the blocks onto the pieces of paper where you think they belong.*
- *Explain how you decided where to put each block.*
- *Tell why it is not easy to decide where to put some blocks.*

- *Look at the number of blocks on each piece of paper.*
- *What do you think this means?*

Ask the child,
- *Look at the tracing of the circle and tell how you think all circles are the same?*
- *How can circles be different?*

Measurement Sense

Children use numbers and number names to examine and identify sets of discrete objects to find the answer to, *how many?*

A system of assigning number names can be used to express the *magnitude* of some *continuous quantities* or *amounts*, and provide the answer to *How much?* according to such questions as: *How long?*; *How tall?*; *How heavy?*; *How big?*; *How fast?*; and *How long does it take?* The *measurement* involved for finding the answers to these questions is a highly complicated process and it is beyond the age range for this book.

As young children examine the world around them and the objects that are in it, they rely heavily on perception. The world to them is as they see it. They see no need for *measurement* of any kind. Children need to learn and know that there are times when things are not as they appear to be, our eyes may deceive us.

The attributes of two objects may differ in appearance yet may be the same. Two differently shaped pieces of cake may contain the same amount of cake.

In contrast, objects that have the same appearance may in fact be quite different. Two identical cubes but made of different materials, one could be light and the other heavy.

These examples illustrate that for comparisons a need to *measure* the attributes of the object or objects that are being compared exists.

The goals of the early stages of learning include defining different characteristics and making *relative comparisons* using appropriate terminology. Children need to be shown that the over used words *big* and *small* are inadequate as well as inappropriate when comparisons are made.

For example, think about a child looking at two pencils on a table, one very long, but thin; the other very thick, but short. The word *big* does not suffice for a task that requires the selection of one of the pencils.

(continued next page ...)

Measurement Sense (cont'd)

**Specific Goals
for
Measurement
Sense**

Children will be able to:
- identify which attribute is to be measured and compared.
- consider both endpoints and everything in between when making *relative comparisons* that involve length and distance.
- use: *as long as, same length, as tall as, same height, as wide, same width, as narrow, long, longer, longest, short, shorter, shortest, tall , taller, tallest, wide, wider, widest, narrow, narrower, narrowest* when describing and making *comparisons* that involve length and height.
- use: *same size, small, smaller, smallest, big, bigger, biggest* when describing and making *comparisons* involving area.
- use: *holds more, holds less, holds the most, holds the least, holds the same amount* when describing and making *comparisons* involving capacity.
- use: *heavy, heavier, heaviest, light, lighter, lightest, just as heavy, just as light* when describing and *comparing* weight (mass).
- use: *takes a long time; takes a longer time; takes the longest time; takes little time; takes less time; takes the least amount of time* when describing and making *comparisons* involving time.
- to tell us that sometimes things may be different from how they appear or what they look like and so we have to check to find out what is true.

Sorting According to Length

Possible Materials:

• One paper plate with a paperclip on it and an empty plate beside it.

• A collection of things, i.e., pieces of string, drinking straws and sticks that can be sorted according to *as long as* the paperclip and *not as long as* the paperclip.

• Two empty paper plates.

A sorting activity is well suited to define for the child what we mean by *length*; *as long as* or *the same length*; and *not as long as*.

Invite the child to,
• *Look at the things and put those that you think are the same length or just as long as the paperclip onto the plate with the paperclip.*
• *Place the things that are not as long as the paperclip onto the other plate.*

After completing the sorting task,
• *How could you show someone that each object is the same length as the paperclip.*

A third plate is introduced. The paperclip is placed onto one plate; one plate is labeled *longer than* and the other *shorter than*.

The child is asked to sort the objects by putting them onto the appropriate plates. Before each placement, ask the child to show that the decision is correct by fitting the objects onto the paperclip. This 'fitting' task defines *length* in terms of the two endpoints and everything in between these two endpoints. Children need to learn that this meaning of *length* is important for making comparisons that involve *lengths*, *distances* or *heights*.

Twisted Strings

Materials:

• Five twisted pieces of string, close to the same length, in different positions.

• Two pieces of string the same length.

Invite the child to,
• *Look at the pieces of string and point to the one that you think might be the longest and then point to the piece that you think could be the shortest.*
• *Why is it not easy to tell?*
• *Show what you would do to put these pieces of string in order from shortest to longest.*
• *Explain what you are thinking as you are trying to put the pieces of string in order.*

Shortest and Tallest

Materials:

- Sketches of four children
  (or trees)
  in order of height
  - two about the same height.

  Beside the tallest,
  a child (tree) shorter
  than the tallest
  standing on a chair (on a hill)
  - the head (crown)
  is above the tallest.

  Beside the shortest
  child (tree), a child kneeling
  (a tree at a slant with
  the crown slightly
  lower than the shortest tree).

  A slanted roof
  with three flag poles equal in
  length on different lower parts
  of the slant part of the roof.

Ask the following questions about the children or the trees.
- *Look at the children. Which one do you think is the tallest child?*
- *How do you know?*
- *Which one do you think is the shortest child? How do you know?*

- *If someone told you that they thought the child standing on the chair is the tallest child, what would you say to them?*

- *What would you say to someone who thought that the child who is kneeling is the shortest child, what would you say to them?*

- *Look at the flagpoles with flags on different parts of the roof.*
- *Which flagpole do you think is the tallest?*
- *Why do you think so?*

- *Which flagpole do you think is the shortest?*
- *Why do you think so?*

- *What do you think we need to do and know before we can tell which of several objects is the tallest and which is the shortest?*

Sorting Rectangles

Materials:

- Several rectangular pieces of paper with one dimension the same, the other slightly different.

- Several pieces of paper the same size and shape.

- Three paper plates with two of them marked with *smaller* and *bigger*, respectively.

Place one of the several pieces that are the same size on the unmarked plate.

- One rectangular piece of paper of different dimensions.

Invite the child to,
- *Find all of the pieces of paper that are the same size and put them onto the same plate.*
- *What can you do to show that they are the same size?*
- *Explain what you are thinking.*

- *Now take all the pieces that are bigger or smaller than these pieces and put these onto the appropriate plates.*

After the sorting is completed ask the child,
- *How can you show that a piece is bigger?*
- *How can you show that a piece is smaller?*

Introduce a piece of rectangular paper of different dimensions and present the problem of determining where the piece belongs and ask,
- *What do you think can be done to find out where this piece belongs?*

Comparing Different Shapes

Materials:

- Three square-shaped
  pieces of paper
  that are the same size.

- One piece is cut in half;
  the two pieces
  are rearranged into
  a rectangular shape.

- One piece is cut diagonally;
  the two pieces
  are rearranged into
  a triangular shape.

Accommodating Responses

Place the three different shapes in front of the child.

Present the child with the scenario of having another child declare that the three 'pieces of cake' are all different in size.

The other child believes that the piece in the shape of a rectangle is the biggest piece.

Pose the following questions,
- *What would you say to this child?*
- *What would you ask this child to do?* or,
- *What could be done to find out whether the statement is true or false?*

If the child thinks that it is not possible for the pieces to be the same size, revisit the setting at a later date after completing and discussing some activities that involve modifying a figure.

For example, the child is given four copies of figures that have the same shape, such as a rectangle, and is requested to,
- *For each rectangle, make no more than two cuts.*
- *Rearrange the pieces of each rectangle into a figure with a new shape.*

After the child examines the new shapes, ask the child,
- *What is different about the figures?*
- *What do you think is the same about the figures?*
- *Explain your thinking.*

Invite the child to,
- *Explain how it is possible to show that the different looking figures are the same size.*

Comparing Containers

Materials:

- Six similar looking glasses
or containers
of different sizes,
two of them almost the
same size,
in random order.

The containers
are labeled A to F.

Place the containers in front of the child, in random order
and invite the child to,
- *Pretend all of the glasses are filled with water.*
- *Look at these glasses.*
- *Which one do you think can hold the most water?*
- *Why do you think so? Explain your thinking.*

- *Which one do you think can hold the least amount of water?
Why do you think so?*
- *Which two do you think could hold about the same amount
of water? Why did you pick these two?*

- *Use the letters to show how you would arrange the glasses
from holding the least to holding the most water.*
- *What could you do to show that your ordering is correct?*

Different, But the Same

Materials:

- As many different types
of containers
that hold one litre
as possible:
milk carton,
yogurt container,
ice cream container,
bottles of different shapes,
vase.

Ask the child,
- *Look at the containers. What do you think is different
about these containers?*
- *Do you think there is anything the same about all of
these containers?*
- *Do you think it is possible that some of these are the
same size or that they can hold the same amount of water?*

Select one container with a label '*one litre*' and tell the child, *the amount
of liquid that fits into this container is called* **one litre**.
- *Look at the different containers.*
- *Do you think it is possible that some of these containers
can hold the same amount of water or one litre?*
Whether the answer is '*yes*' or '*no*', the child is asked to explain what
might be done to show that the given answer is correct.

For some children this idea has to be revisited at a later date after many
experiences of comparing containers by pouring sand, small pebbles or
water.

Explaining Up and Down

Materials:

- Sketches of six see-saws.

  - *First see-saw*:
  not level with two children
  (stick people).

  - *Second see-saw*:
  two children at the same level.

  - *Third see-saw*:
  not level with two boxes,
  the smaller box at the lower end.

  - *Fourth see-saw*:
  level with two similar looking
  boxes of different sizes.

  - *Fifth see-saw*:
  not level with two
  identical boxes.

  - *Sixth* see-saw:
  level with two children,
  one of them is holding
  a small box or an animal.

Accommodating Responses

Present the sketches one at a time. First see-saw:
- *What do we know and what can we say about each of the two children when the see-saw is not level?*

The child may need reminders to make comparison comments about both of the children and later about both of the boxes.

Second see-saw:
- *What do we know and what can we say about each of the two children when the see-saw is level?*

Third see-saw:
- *If a smaller box is on the side that is lower down, what can you say about the boxes?*

Fourth see-saw:
- *If two boxes that are different in size are on a see-saw that is level, what can you say about the boxes?*

Fifth see-saw:
- *If two boxes of the same size are on a see-saw that is level, what can you say about the boxes?*

Sixth see-saw:
- *If two children are on a see-saw that is level and one of the children is holding a box or an animal, what do you think we know about the two children?*

As the child explains what can be said about each of the two children or boxes, elicit a suggestion about what might be inside the boxes to make what is shown possible.

If, by chance, the child suggests that the illustrated outcomes are not possible, return to the pictures at a later time after the completion of further activities involving comparisons.

They Look the Same, But?

Possible Materials:

- Five containers of the same size and shape.

  For example:
  small film canisters,
  filled with different amounts
  of sand.

Two containers hold the same amount of sand.

Accommodating Responses

Use objects from around the room and then invite the child to,
- *Think of something that is heavy.*
- *Now name something that is heavier than that.*
- *What would something even heavier than that be?*

- *As you hear each of the words: heavy, heavier, and heaviest, say the names of the things you found or suggested.*

- *Now pick out or think of something that you think is light.*
- *What would be lighter than that?*
- *What is even lighter than that?*

- *As you hear each of the words: light, lighter, lightest, say the names of the things you found or suggested.*

- *Look at the containers.*
  - *They look the same, but they contain different things.*
  - *Two of them are the same, but the others are different.*

- *Tell me what you think you could do to:*
  - *find the lightest container.*
  - *find the heaviest container.*
  - *find the two that weigh the same.*
  - *put them in order from light to heavy.*
- *Explain your thinking.*

If the child suggests the use of a see-saw or a scale, make the request to suggest how it might be done without these instruments.

If the level of difficulty for the five containers is too challenging for a child, present a problem for three containers that are filled with different amounts of sand.

At an even simpler stage, present pairs of containers filled with different amounts of sand for comparison and description.

It might be suggested to the child to use two hands to model a see-saw.

Takes More or Less Time?

Possible Materials:

- Sketches of pairs of frames, and one set of three frames, showing simple actions that a child is familiar with.

- Examples of pairs of frames:
  - child combing hair -
  giving a dog a bath
  - brushing teeth
  - washing dishes in a sink.

- Three frames showing:
  putting on a hat
  - tying shoes
  - washing a bicycle.

If sketches are not available, describe these actions and invite the child to do a little pantomime or acting.

Request the child to,
- *Think of activities that are done around the home.*
- *Give examples of events that you think take a long time to do.*
- *Which of the activities you have suggested takes the longest time to complete?*

- *Think of activities that are done around the home.*
- *Give examples of things that you think take little time to do.*
- *Which of the activities you have suggested takes the least amount of time to complete?*

Name two events that involve actions.
For example: ***taking out the garbage***   ***taking a bath***

Ask the child,
- *Pretend you are doing both of these tasks, which of the two do you think takes longer or more time to do? Explain your thinking.*

Ask the child,
- *Could it be possible for the other task to take more time?*
Depending on the answer, it is followed with *Why?* or *Why not?*

Ask the child to look at the pairs of frames, one pair at a time.
- *Explain the actions that are illustrated.*
- *Which of the two actions do you think takes less time to complete?*

Again ask the child,
- *Do you think another answer is possible? Why? or, Why not?*

Present the three frames. Request the child to,
- *Explain the actions that are illustrated in each of the three drawings.*
- *Try to order the three actions shown in the drawings from takes little time to complete to takes the longest time to complete.*

Follow this with,
- *Do you think the three actions could be put into a different order? Why? or, Why not?*

Record Sheet Suggestions

Do the responses uttered by a child yield any indicators of the development of *spatial sense* (visualization) or *measurement sense* (my eyes may deceive me)? Is the language the child uses to describe parts of blocks and different attributes of objects while making comparisons appropriate and correct?

1. Explanations that indicate an awareness of, *the view-point determines what a block reminds me of* – **What does it Look Like?**

   _____

   _____

2. Explanations indicating how a *three-dimensional object*, or a block, was selected from a set of objects to be a *matched with a diagram or photograph* of the object – **Try to Match It; See and Cannot See**.

   _____

   _____

3. Explanations indicating an understanding of the fact that *more than one view is required* to ensure that a copy of a given structure can be made – **See and Cannot See – Drawings**.

   _____

   _____

4. Comments about *faces*, *edges* or *corners* suggestive of knowing that *blocks which look different can in some ways be the same* – **Face Count**.

   _____

   _____

5. Comments suggestive of an awareness of *faces, edges and corners* while attempting to identify blocks that are the same, or are similar, during a *tactile activity* – **Feel It and Try to Tell**.

   _____

   _____

6. Explanations indicating an awareness of the number of *faces, edges* and *corners* that are not visible and the *possibility that more than one answer* exists when attempting to match a block with a diagram – **See and Cannot See – Drawings**.

   _____

   _____

(continued next page ...)

Record Sheet Suggestions (cont'd)

7. Responses indicating an ability to consider *two or more attributes* of a block at the same time – **Two Difference Train**.

_____

_____

8. Comments indicating an awareness of the parts of a triangle (rectangle; circle) and of how all triangles (rectangles; circles) are the same and how they can differ.

_____

_____

9. Appropriate use of *comparison language* for: length or height; area; capacity; weight (mass); time.

_____

_____

10. Examples of responses indicating an awareness that sometimes *our eyes deceive us* – **Twisted Strings; Sorting Different Shapes; Different, But the Same; Explaining Up and Down; They look the Same, But?**

_____

_____

11. Indicators of *confidence, willingness to take risks* and *tolerance for ambiguity*.

_____

_____

Problem Solving

Problem solving is what happens and what is done when encountering a situation where one does not know what to do. *Problem solving* is connecting and applying one's knowledge to new or novel situations, or in new ways to familiar settings. *Problem solving* also includes re-inventing or re-constructing something that has been forgotten.

Problem solving needs to be part of an ongoing approach or procedure. Trying to deal with *problem solving* as a separate entity, or telling children how to solve a problem, giving them a plan to solve a problem, or providing key words or hints, is unlikely to help them become *successful problem solvers*.

Sense-making, or having everything *make sense,* is a requisite *for problem solving*. Without a *sense of number* and without *spatial sense* it is unlikely that the goal of *fostering problem solving ability* can be reached. This *sense-making* is a key component of the activities illustrated in this book. However, the activities alone do not suffice. The *type of questions*, the *accommodation of all answers,* and the *conversations* that are suggested and are part of the activities are of prime importance. The *orchestration* of the activities provides the key component for teaching the child *via* or *through problem solving.*

To illustrate and reinforce the importance of *questioning strategies,* the *key questions* that were part of many of the activities are revisited.

General Goals for Problem Solving

Since *problem solving* is not developed in an isolated setting, it does not make sense to suggest specific goals. However, there exist some distinguishing characteristics of children who are successful problem solvers. These characteristics were kept in mind when tasks and activity settings were designed.

Successful problem solvers note likenesses and differences.
Sorting and *classifying* have been identified as important mental activities. These are not just part of *readiness settings* but an aspect of *number sense, spatial sense, measurement sense* as well as other areas of sense making in mathematics.

Successful problem solvers have the ability to visualize.
Visualization is essential to making *sense of numbers*. Activities that get children to: recognize number *without counting* (subetizing); think about numbers when hearing number names or seeing numerals; and think of different ways of showing the same number all demand *visualization.*

(continued next page ...)

General Goals for Problem Solving
(cont'd)

Spatial sense activities included looking at blocks from different view-points, matching blocks with pictures of blocks and trying to describe the parts that can be seen and trying to make predictions about the parts that cannot be seen. These tasks along with the attempt to try and have children consider more than one possible response for one prompt all involve *visualization*.

Successful problem solvers generalize on the basis of a few examples. Generalizations and testing generalizations are essential aspects of mathematics. Occasions for introducing generalizations to making and applying them happen when the simple properties for the *basic addition* and *basic subtraction facts* are discussed and examined.

Successful problem solvers understand mathematical terms and ideas. It makes no sense to ask children to memorize terms and ideas for the sake of doing so. One way to foster understanding is by the children's use of familiar language and using it in conjunction with mathematical terminology. This strategy is illustrated when children are introduced to *addition* and *subtraction*.

Successful problem solvers make connections.
Connecting what is learned to settings outside the classroom, to previous learning and to ongoing learning is one aspect of problem solving strategy and is indicative of understanding what is learned. Connecting is fostered when the materials that are used for activities are familiar to children and familiar language is used to introduce mathematical ideas and terminology.

Successful problem solvers are able to estimate.
The difference between guessing and *estimating* is explained to children. For example, when looking at numbers, children learn to use the *referents* five and ten to arrive at estimates.

Successful problem solvers are willing to switch or try new methods.
Fostering this quality of problem solving requires the accommodation of all responses. Young children can learn that often there is more than one way of doing things and there may exist different answers for a given question or problem. The specific examples in this chapter illustrate the strategies and types of questions that are used throughout the book in an attempt to create favourable settings for reaching this goal.

Successful problem solvers are confident.
Having a high self esteem results in children *taking risks* - cognitive risks. This is essential for knowing when to switch or devise new methods; for *asking questions;* for accepting that responses from others can also be correct and acceptable; and for being willing and able to use one's own language to talk about what is learned in one's own words.

Self esteem is encouraged in settings where responses are considered as being more than right or wrong; where all explanations are valued and discussed; and where the emphasis is not on reciting or repeating ideas in a specified way.

(continued next page ...)

Selective Strategies for Presenting Mathematical Ideas *via* Problem Solving

The types of questions asked are critical in fostering problem solving ability *via* or *through problem solving*. The accommodation of the answers that children provide requires careful attention and a special skill. Children are not just *invited to think*, but whenever possible *flexible thinking* and *advancing thinking* are also part of this setting.

Since the qualities for successful problem solving are dependent upon a skilful orchestration of conversations and an ability to accommodate all types of responses from children, it is easy to see why computer or textbook learning is ineffective and insufficient.

The types of activities that follow have been presented earlier. The intent here is to illustrate teaching children *via* or *through problem solving*. To reach this goal, the types of questions and strategies that accommodate the possible answers that are uttered by children are revisited.

Problem solving can be part of the presentation of new ideas. Special time need not be set aside for problem solving since it is already part of the child's mathematics learning. In a preschool setting questions can be posed as children are engaged in free play or whenever the opportunity arises.

For example, in one pre-school building material was available. A piece of wood was used for an incline or hill. The children were asked to build something that could roll down the hill. The question, *I wonder how far it would roll?* gave rise to interesting speculations and corresponding placements of markers. It was somewhat predictable for young children to replace these markers to wherever their constructions stopped.

Then the following challenge was presented, *How could you change part of what you have built to make it roll farther?* The children who explained their reasons were serious and thought these to be sensible. To an adult, however, these responses may be quite amusing.

For example, who could argue with, *'Wings help birds and that is why they will help cars'* and, *'Making it longer will make it go faster.'*

Some children even ventured a guess about how much further the modified vehicle might roll. Discrepancies between the new guess and the result were fixed by most children by quickly adjusting the markers.

In one setting children were building with blocks. One child made a tower. The children were presented with the challenge of using different blocks and building other towers just as tall; some on different levels, i.e., on a chair and on a table. Upon completion, they were invited to somehow show that these towers were just as tall. The children's attempts to show that the towers were the same height involved a variety of problem solving strategies. Some of these were unique. A few were a little amusing to an adult, but not to the child.

Sorting and Classifying

Possible Materials:

- Four different toy wild animals or sketches of animals.

For example:
anteater;
kangaroo;
alligator;
male lion.

Present the animals and make the request,

- *Look at the animals.*
- *How do you think these animals are in some way the same?*
  or,
- *Think of all of the things you can think of that is the same for these animals.*

Accommodating Responses

If the approach appears too *open-ended,* inviting the child to look at a certain target area may be required before noticing some common characteristics.
For example,

- *Look at the heads or the back ends and try to tell how these animals are in some way the same.*

If as part of *documentation,* a list of the child's responses is kept, it can be returned to at different intervals to see if the child goes beyond what has been discussed.
For example,

- *So far you have said that they have two eyes, two ears, a long tail and four legs.*
- *Try to spy, with your little eye, some other things that are the same.*

If the child comes up with more examples these are added to the *documentation.*

The final list of a child's responses can be used to introduce the next task.

- *You have come up with all of these things that tell how the animals are in some way the same* (the list is read to the child), *now look at the animals and pick out one that you think is in some way different or does not belong.*
- *Explain how it is different?*

- *You said '...' is different because '...', now try to think of another animal that is in some way different or could not belong. How is it different?*

The child's identification of two or more members of the group as different indicates *thinking flexibly.*

(continued next page ...)

Key Ideas and Questions – Selective Activities – Via Problem Solving

Accommodating Responses
(cont'd)

If a child does not identify a second animal as *different*, identify one animal by pointing to and announcing,

- *I think this one is in some way different.*
  Try to guess what I might be thinking of?

A few hints may be necessary.

Vary the setting by having the child look at a collection, in this case toy wild animals, and ask the child to select four that are in some way the same.

- *Tell how the animals you have selected are in some*
  way the same.

Then ask the child to examine these four animals several times in terms of,

- *Which one of these four do you think is in some way different?*

As in previous tasks, *documentation* is important to *advancing children's thinking*. After the child sorts a set of animals into two groups such as, *'these are all wild animals'* and *'these are not wild'*, take a digital photograph. Ask the child to think of another way of sorting the same animals. Again take a photograph. Revisit the task on a different day and begin with a look at the photographs.

- *This is what you did last time* (the categories are described).
- *Today try to think of still other ways of sorting the same animals.*

Creating the new classes becomes part of the *documentation* as one piece of evidence of *advanced thinking* and perhaps a starting point for future tasks.

Ordering

Possible Materials:

• Duplicates
of four simple sketches:
- stick person by fire pit.
- stick person by tent,
(hand on tent).
- stick person
walking toward car,
(something in hand).
- stick person walking with
something in arms.

Or,
- a stick person flying a kite.
- a stick person
walking with a kite.
- a stick person and a kite
on the ground some
distance away.
- a stick person standing
by a house with kite under
the arm and a cloud
in the sky.

Accommodating Responses

Give the four sketches to the child and make the requests,
- *Identify the picture that you think comes first and the picture that you think comes last.*
- *Explain your thinking.*
- *Now try to tell a story about the four pictures and put them in the order of your story.*

Create *documentation* by pasting the pictures as ordered onto a sheet of paper. Record the story below the pictures.

If several copies of the pictures are prepared, there is no need to take a photograph.

Put aside the first sequence and story. Present the four sketches again with the request,
- *Try to tell a different story for the pictures.*

You might suggest to the child,
- *Try to think of another picture that you think could come first. If 'this' (a sketch is pointed to) comes first, what could your story be now?*

If the child does not make up a second story or declares it not possible, make the request,
- *Try to explain your thinking.*

Present a different sequence to the child with the explanation,
- *Somebody put the pictures in this order.*
- *Try to guess what story this child might have been thinking of.*

If the child makes up a story to match this sequence, the following questions are posed,
- *Does this story make sense to you?*
- *Why?* or, *Why not?*

Thinking About Patterns

Possible Materials:

- A simple repeating pattern
  or
  a drawing of the pattern.

  For example:
  bolt - washer - nut -
  bolt - washer - nut.

  Or,
  with toy animals:
  duck - chicken - goose.

  Or,
  with three different objects:
  button - paperclip - bottle cap.

Accommodating Responses

Challenge the child to,

- *Try and think of all of the different things that you think could come next.*
- *Explain the reason or reasons for selecting and placing the object or objects.*

Prepare sketches or lists to *document* each different suggestion.

If this challenge is too *open-ended* for a child, the following suggestions can be made.

If the child continues a repeating pattern ask,

- *Do you think it is possible to change this into a different repeating pattern than the one you have made?*

Follow a positive response with,

- *Explain the new pattern.*
- *Do you think another repeating pattern is possible?*

Then request,

- *Try to think of a way to change the repeating pattern into a growing pattern.*

Accommodate a positive response in one of two ways.
For one, make the request,

- *Try and think of a different type of growing pattern.*

Or, make the request,

- *Look at the growing pattern you have made and try to change it into a repeating pattern.*

Numbers and Number Names

Problem solving and some characteristics of successful problem solvers are accommodated when children respond to requests like,

- *Use your fingers to show a number in a different way* and,
- *Look at the fingers that were flashed. How many do you think you saw and how many do you think you did not see?*

Different Names for Numbers

Possible Materials:

- Sketches of:
A pair of balloons
tied together and eight
happy faces.

Or,
two pieces of paper
that serve as pens
and eight toy animals.

Or,
two paper plates and eight
counters that serve as cookies.

- Pieces of paper for
documentation:
recordings of sketches
and the number names for
each different response.

Create a problem setting by inviting the child to,

- *Try to think of and show all of the different ways of how eight happy faces can be placed onto two balloons* (or placing eight animals into two pens; or placing eight cookies onto two plates).

Present the follow-up questions as further challenges,

- *What is the same about the happy faces on each pair of balloons? What is different?*
- *How could you find out, or how do you know you have shown all of the possible different ways of putting eight happy faces onto two balloons?*

Different Ways to Show Numbers

Materials:

- Dimes and pennies.

- Pairs of boxes;
  or circles drawn
  on a piece of paper;
  or paper plates labelled:
  dimes   pennies.

- A piece of paper
  for the documentation
  of each response.

Accommodating Responses

Present a two-digit numeral (42, 36, ...) and invite the child to,
- *Use dimes and pennies and try to show the meaning of forty-two (thirty-six, ...) in as many different ways as possible.*

Prepare a sketch as a record of each response.

After several recordings, ask the child,
- *What is different about the recordings?*
- *What do you think is the same about the recordings?*

Keep in mind that more than one answer is possible to the last question and redirection might be necessary for the child to conclude that, *'there are different ways of showing the same number'* (amount of money).

Ask the child,
- *Do you know of a way of telling whether you have shown all of the possible ways?*
- *Why? or, Why not?*

Patterns with Number Names

Materials:

• Numerals recorded on cards: two of each **0** to **9**.

Create a problem solving setting by integrating an *open-ended* task, similar to the one for ***Thinking about Patterns,*** with a request for sequences with numerals.

For example,
Present one of the following sequences to the child:

1 - 2 - 3 - [ ]   2 - 4 - 6 - [ ]

For each of the sequences, invite the child to respond to,
• *Try to think of all of the different number names that you think could come next.*
• *Explain your thinking for each answer.*
• *Do you think any other number names could come next?*
• *Explain your thinking.*

The types of questions asked next and strategies for accommodating the different responses are the same as for ***Thinking about Patterns.***

Use the *documentation* of a child's responses to collect information about *risk taking* and aspects of *thinking* when similar tasks are presented in the future.

Writing Hints about a Number or a Number Name

Writing hints for a mystery number name, revising the hints, realizing that more hints are required, or that some hints are redundant is part of problem solving as well as language development and reading comprehension.

For a **Money Mystery** setting, ask the child to think of dimes and pennies and an amount of money less than one dollar. Write or tell some hints about the amount of money you are thinking of. Let somebody try to guess the amount of money.

After the child records hints for a mystery amount of money, or these are recorded for the child, pose the following questions:
- *If you think there is one hint that is more (less) important than the other hints, which one do you select?*
- *Why do you think this hint is more (less) important?*

Rather than talking about importance, ask the questions,
- *Which hint gives someone the most information about your mystery amount of money? Why do you think that is the case?*
- *Which hint gives someone the least or very little information about your mystery amount of money? Why do you think that is the case?*

Operations – Creating Problems

When asking children to make up and write their own problems they problem solve by *connecting* numbers, relations and operations to events and action to their experience. This type of an activity enhances *problem solving ability*.

Asking children to make up problems for diagrams depicting the *additive* or the *subtractive actions* is problem solving that provides insight into their *understanding*.
The problems children create indicate whether they correctly describe:
- the numbers;
- the action;
- or both, the numbers and the action.

When children are asked to make up problems for equations some children may not know what is meant by *making up a problem*, especially if they have not done this before. For these children the request needs to be changed to, *Try to make up a story*. However, when some children hear the word *story*, they can get carried away and some redirection may be required.

The need for redirection is illustrated by the following sample response.

For **8 - 3 = [ ]** one young girl responded with,
Once upon a time there was an eight. He was walking in the forest. And then he saw a 'm' in the bush, but when he looked closely it was a three lying down. So they climbed a tree and said, "Let's take away". There were some eggs in the tree and they sat on them. Suddenly they hatched and all the numbers came out.

Who says equations are boring?

Mental Mathematics Strategies

Equations are presented.

    For example: **7 + 8 = 15**   **13 ÷ 6 = 7**

The child is requested to,

- *Explain as many different ways as you can, other than counting by ones, that the answer is correct.*
- *Try to show each of your ways with counters.*

Present an equation to the child.

    For example: **9 = [ ] + [ ]**   **12 = [ ] + [ ]**

Invite the child to,

- *Think of all of the possible number names that would make the equation true.*
- *Explain and use counters to show that your equations are true.*

Keep a record of each response.

- *Do you think you have included all of the possible number names?*

If the answer is, *'yes'*,

- *How do you know or why do you think so?*

If the answer is *'no'*,

- *Why did you say that?*

For an equation like: **9 = [ ] + [ ] + [ ]**, ask the child to,

- *Explain how you would figure out how to find the missing number names for this equation?*

- *Try to write as many different true equations as you can think of.*

- *Do you know of any way of checking or finding out whether you found all the possible number names for this equation?*

Spatial Sense

Possible Materials:

- Sketch or photograph
of a frontal view
of a construction made from
several blocks.

- Or, a building made
from several different blocks
on a window ledge
or on a cabinet.

- A collection of blocks,
with duplicates and
similar blocks.

- Wooden puzzle
with several pieces
to create one object
or one animal.

- Wooden puzzle
– whole objects or animals
are placed
into openings of the outlines
of these objects or animals.

Visual imagery and *visual thinking* are important aspects of *spatial sense*.

Present the photograph and ask,
- *Why do you think it is not possible to tell how many blocks were used for constructing this building?*

Asking the child to make a construction of what is featured in the picture by using several different blocks requires the use of several thinking strategies. The examination of a photograph and the selection of blocks involves *matching* and *sorting*. The actual building requires *ordering*.
- *Pretend there are no hidden blocks.*
- *Try to construct a building that is like the one in the drawing, but make it smaller.*
- *Explain what you are thinking as you pick out blocks and as you are putting up your building.*
- *How are the two buildings the same?*
- *How are the two buildings different?*

Ask the same questions after a requesting the child to,
- *Try to construct a building that is like the one in the drawing, but is bigger.*
- *Explain what you are thinking as you pick out blocks and begin to build.*

Make the request to,
- *Construct a building that is completely different from the one in the picture.*
- *Explain what you are thinking as you are picking out blocks and as you are putting up your building.*
- *What are all of the things that are different?*
- *Do you think there is anything that is the same for the two buildings?*

For a wooden puzzle in one frame with several pieces, challenge the child to,
- *Try and put the puzzle pieces together outside the frame.*
- *Explain what you are doing and how you are deciding where to put the pieces.*

Make the request to use the puzzle pieces and,
- *Try and put the puzzle together outside the frame and upside down.*
- *Explain what you are trying to do and how you decide on where to place the pieces.*

If the child is successful, point to a piece and ask the child to predict what might be shown on the other side and give reasons for the response.

(continued next page ...)

Spatial Sense (cont'd)

Ask the child to place the hands behind the back. After the child closes the eyes, place one piece of the puzzle into the hands. Invite the child to,

- *Feel the piece and all around it.*
- *Try to guess which part of the puzzle you think you have in your hands.*

If the answer is correct,

- *How did you know what to say?*

If the child is unable to respond,

- *Why do you think this cannot be done?*

Different types of wooden puzzles allow for different levels of difficulties for this type of tactile task. A puzzle that requires the placement of different types of animals or objects into their respective frames is easier than considering a part of a puzzle consisting of many pieces when attempts are made to identify a piece behind the back.

No matter what the setting, many young children find it rather difficult to resist peeking into a hand behind the back as part of a solution strategy. If nothing else, this strategy builds confidence.

For a lead-up task for the animals and objects type puzzles, place the pieces in front of the child in a face down position.
Present one piece to the child and make the following requests,

- *What animal do you think is painted on the other side of this piece?*
- *Which part of the piece helped you with your answer?* or, *Explain your thinking.*

Point to one end of the puzzle piece and ask the child,

- *What do you think is painted on the other side of this part of the piece?*
- *How did you know what to say?*

The strategy could be changed to,

- *Point to where you would paint the head and face of the animal.*
- *Why would you paint it there?*

Measurement Sense

Possible Materials:

• Sketch of a see-saw, level – with two similar boxes of different sizes.

• Sketch of a see-saw, not level – with the same type of boxes; the smaller box on the lower part.

• A sketch of four similar looking boxes of different sizes.

• Two copies of three sketches of three activities arranged in two different ways.

For example:
- brushing teeth
- tying a shoe
- combing hair.
If sketches are not available, the suggested actions can be described to the child.

Present the sketch of the level see-saw showing two boxes that look similar but differ in size and ask,
  • *Do you think this is possible?* If the answer is, *'Yes', How could you explain this?* and,
  • *What do you think you know about the boxes and what is in them?*
If the answer is, *'No', Why not?*

Present the sketch with the see-saw not level; the smaller box at the lower end and ask,
  • *Do you think this is possible?*
If the answer is, *'Yes', How could you explain this?* and,
  • *What do you think you know about the boxes and what is in them?*
If the answer is, *'No', Why not?*

Present the sketch of the four similar boxes of different sizes and make the requests,
  • *Let's pretend there are presents in these boxes.*

Children are allowed to choose one of the boxes.
  • *What would you tell the children who say, I will always choose the biggest box.*
  • *Explain why you would say that.*

Invite the child to,
  • *Name something that you think takes a long time to do or complete.*
  • *Name something that you think takes little time to do or complete.*

Tell the child that two children answered the question, *Which takes longer to complete, feeding the cat or making your bed?* in different ways. Challenge the child with,
  • *Try to explain how it might be possible that both children's answers are correct.*

Tell the child, *Two children came up with different answers for arranging:* **brushing teeth – tying a shoe – combing hair** *from 'it takes little time' to 'it takes a long time' to complete.*
  • *Which of these two children's sequences do you agree with? Why?*
  • *Do you think the other sequence is incorrect? Why or why not?*
  • *If a child said to you that another sequence is possible, what would you say to that child? Why would you say that?*

Games and Game Settings

Appropriate game settings, or in this case age-appropriate game settings, present an opportunity to create an environment that accommodates important aspects of mathematics learning or *numeracy*.

If the game settings are age-appropriate, the emphasis is not on winning, on being first, on being fastest, or on being smartest. Appropriate settings provide opportunities for *imagination* and for *spontaneous invention*. These settings maintain and foster the development of important characteristics of good problem solvers which include: a *can-do attitude*, *confidence* and *risk taking*. As will become evident, other general goals that were stated for problem solving are also achieved in these settings.

Game settings provide opportunities for children to be active, to talk, to think, to revise and advance their thinking.

One of the greatest values of playing games lies in the conversations that take place while the games are played. As children talk, opportunities arise for them to explain their thinking about a move they have made, or how a move may affect the outcome of a game.

Documentation plays an important role in *advancing children's thinking* in settings that involve the playing of games. Any comments that children make while playing a game should be recorded.

When the game setting is revisited, these comments serve as a starting point reminding the child of suggestions previously made and what was done the last time the game was played.

Commercial Game Settings

Possible Materials:

• Any commercial game
or game board
from around the house.

For example:
Checkers;
Snake and Ladders;
Chess;
Backgammon.

At a young age, many children believe they know how to do everything. Children who have never cooked will not only tell how to prepare their favourite meals, but will also suggest the ingredients they think should be part of the meal. Some of the ingredients they include as part of their explanations may have nothing to do with the mentioned meal.

This confidence is also evident when young children are asked about games or game boards they have only seen. Having never played a game before does not stop these children from sharing the rules they think are or should be part of a game.

The intent of the suggested setting is to take advantage of children's self-confidence and to let them be in charge. This gives them an opportunity to *talk*, to *invent*, to *use imagination* - to *be happy*.

Orchestrating the playing of a game according to a child's rules is not demanding. The main tasks include observing, listening, and accepting whatever the child suggests, and keeping notes as part of the *documentation*. These notes can be used at a later date as a reminder when playing the game again and extending or revising the rules that had been suggested.

The suggested procedure is simple. Present a game board and the pieces that go with it to a child and ask,
  • *Do you know how to play this game and do you know
    the rules or some of the rules?*

The amazing thing is that many children will respond with, *'yes.'*
If this is the case, make the request,
  • *Explain how you think the game is played and I will
    play it with you.*

Assume the role of the other player and record the rules that the child generates and explains.

If the child responds to the question in a negative way, invite the child to,
  • *Try and make up some rules that you think are part
    or could be part of the game.*

Often young children design games that differ from how an adult views a game. One girl hid her own coloured pegs for *Master Mind* and was happy to try and 'guess'what she had hidden for herself. Success builds confidence!

(continued next page ...)

Other children can become distracted by a comment, a move or a physical characteristic of the setting. These distractions can turn their game into a free-play ritual where an opponent's role changes from that of a participant to that of a soon-forgotten observer.

It is predictable that for most young children the opportunity to be in charge results in rules that ensure that they cannot lose. For young children, this is simply where they are in their thinking.

The explanations of a *Chess* game by a five-year old included the instructions that like pieces can knock one another off the board. For example, *'horses knock off horses'*; *'ashtrays knock off ashtrays'*; and *'baubles knock off baubles.'*

After the partner knocked off a few pieces, the rule, *'And when you feel like it, you can put some back on the board again'* was introduced. The next comment shows how completely in charge he was. The opponent's move to place a piece back onto the board was met with the comment, *'You don't feel like it.'*

These unique rules indicate both, *imagination* and *invention*. They are indicative of a *can-do attitude* and a *high level of self confidence,* desirable for every child! Even if the outcome of playing a game with this child is predictable, he can be challenged to go beyond his initial rules and make new suggestions for the next time the game is played.

Inventing Games

Possible Materials:

- An *open-ended* request simply asks children to consider and choose anything that is available in the immediate environment, make up a game for it, and explain how it is played.

  For example:
  - toy animals and a small box or a small area rug.
  - a collection of blocks and toy cars.
  - coloured chips and paper plates.

- Piece of coloured cardboard or paper and pens of different colours.

Orchestrating this setting is as simple as the previous one. The main tasks include making a suggestion to the child and then observing, listening, accepting what the child suggests, and *documenting* this by keeping notes .

Present the child with a request of the following type,
- *Try to make up a game for these toy animals and this piece of cardboard (or the rug). Think about a farm or a zoo. What rules would you make up for your game?*

Many children will start out by volunteering instructions they identify as their rules, but it may not take long before the setting turns into a free play affair. There will be times when the person who initiated the setting is forgotten and the child continues in a world of solitary play.

The request for rules is many times met with simple instructions like, *'this is how it goes'; 'because that is how it is done'*; and perhaps nothing more than, *'to have fun.'*

The comments children make provide insight into: their understanding of rules; their definition of what a game is; and the role of rules as part of a game - insights and understandings that are often likely to be quite different from that of older children or adults.

After a six-year old girl chose plastic chips of her favourite colour, she was asked to make up a game for these chips. She designed a game board by scribbling thirty-three oval-shaped figures on a piece of writing paper. On another sheet of paper she printed and numbered five rules:
1) *Place the chip(s) on the mat.*
2) *Mix the chips.*
3) *Pick up a chip with your eyes closed.*
4) *You get 1 point when you get it right.*
5) *When you get five Points you win.*

Tally marks were drawn to show how to keep score.

If the rules of this game are followed, everybody is a winner. From the setting and rules she created it can be concluded that she met several of the goals for problem solving by the simple request to make up a game.

(continued next page ...)

For his game, a five-year old boy who did not know how to print, selected plastic chips and two pieces of paper showing ten rectangular regions. His explanations of the rules included references to:
- *each man* (chip) *having three lives.*
- *alligators.*
- *changing colour.*
- *taking chips off and starting over.*

The boy made the comments, *'I am making up rules as I go - sort of';* *'I love this game';* and, *'I love that move - it's cool.'*

Even if an observer of this setting concludes that some of the explanations and rules are too difficult to follow, the value of this type of an activity is illustrated, namely *use of imagination* and *spontaneous invention.*

Aside from the fact that these children felt important when they talked about their games and their rules, *documenting* what they have created allows for an opportunity for future reflection, conversations and going beyond what was created.

Many children enjoy making up a name for their game. Asking children to think about the first important thing they might say to someone who is playing their game, provides a further opportunity for reflection. Some responses to this request are fascinating and a little amusing.

Sample titles:
   Adventure; Pick it; Family Game.

Sample introductory comments – to the point:
   Try to do it right; Don't be a poor sport or you are out;
   Don't cheat - have fun - if you are uncomfortable, please tell
   someone; No peeking - no asking for clues and no fooling around;
   The idea of the game is not to punch people, not to push people,
   not to scream at people.

Games for Numbers and Number Names

What is a Game?   What is a Good Game?

Materials for Playing Games:

- Cubes with numbers
  and
  number names.

  Homemade number
  and
  numeral cubes
  are easy to prepare.

  Shops that deal in
  foam rubber will
  cut remnants
  into small cubes.

Desirable ranges of numerals,
and ranges of different
arrangements of numbers
can be placed on the faces
of these cubes,
and presto a set of noiseless
cubes is available.

What is a game?

Some authors, including those who write materials for the mathematics classroom, take advantage of the popularity and intrinsic value of games by publishing certain types of practice activities within a game context. Many of those who write educational materials often use the term 'games' very loosely to refer to diversions of different kinds. Assigning the label 'game' to an ordinary activity does not seem fair, especially if it is done for the sole purpose of motivation. To be consistent with children's experiences and understanding of what a game is, there should be rules and there should be a winner, winners or a reward of some sort. However, the emphasis should not be on winning.

What is a good game?

Some criteria for good games that are appropriate for young children include:

- the rules should be simple;
- there should be quick action;
- the setting should be simple and few pieces should be required;
- the emphasis should not be on winning;
- it should be a learning experience – corrections should be possible; turns should not be missed; and dropping out of a game should not be a possibility;
- discussions during a game which reinforce what is being learned or are part of decision making should be part of the game;
- winning should be a chance outcome; everyone has an equal chance of winning. This idea can be reinforced by using the word *Lucky* in front of the name for every game. Outcomes of games can then be discussed in terms of *very* or *most lucky*, and *not quite so lucky*.

It is unlikely that the examples included meet all of the criteria of a good game; but the more criteria are met, the better the game. If the suggested discussions for a game involve reflection or decision making, it is likely that many aspects of problem solving are accommodated.

Lucky – To and From Ten

Materials:

• Two cardboard strip game boards, each marked off into ten square spaces in a row.

The squares are big enough to allow for the placement of a button, bottle top or chip.

• A number cube:
- two faces show the number one.
- two faces show the number two.
- two faces show the number three.

The goal of the game is to find out who is lucky to be the first to cover all ten spaces of the game board with chips: **Lucky to Ten**. Players take turns rolling the number cube. The number on the face of the cube tells how many chips can be placed onto the game board.

To illustrate the importance of the conversations during the game, consider the following stage of a game in progress:

Player A has seven chips on the game board, and player B has four chips on it.

The players are asked to respond to types of requests like:
- *Who is ahead?*
- *Show with your fingers how far ahead player A is.*
- *Show with your fingers how many more player A needs to go to ten or to cover all ten spaces.*
- *Show with your fingers how far behind player B is.*
- *Show with your fingers how many more player B needs to go ten or to cover all ten spaces.*

After each turn, ask the players,
• *How far behind (or ahead) are you?*
• *How many more to cover ten squares?*

Possible response options include:
- showing the number with fingers.
- showing the number with fingers and stating the number name.
- stating the number name.

Toward the end of a game a problem needs to be solved.
- What should happen in order to cover the last space or spaces?
- Should players wait for the number on the cube to match the number of empty squares on the board, or would a number on the cube greater than the number of these squares suffice?
The children can decide what they think should be done.

Give children the opportunity to make up a name for the game.

After one player was lucky to be first to cover the ten spaces the first lucky winner, give the second player the opportunity to cover all of the spaces, and to be the second winner.

(continued next page ...)

The goal of the game now changes to:
- Who will be lucky or be the first lucky winner to take off all of the chips?
  Lucky from Ten or **Lucky to Zero**.

The types of questions after every move can be:
- *Who is closer to having zero chips on the board?*
- *How far ahead (behind) ...?*
- *How many have been taken off?*
- *How many more need to be taken off?*

The children can decide on the procedure to follow for taking the last chips off the game board.

When two children play the game on their own, request that they ask each other questions about:
- *how far ahead (behind)* and,
- *how many more to go to ten (zero)*, as the game moves along.

For variations, different number cubes can be used.

For example, mark the faces with numbers from zero to four, with two of the latter; or put number names on the faces.

Lucky Guess and Lucky Guesses

Materials:

- For **Lucky Guess**,
  a game sheet:
  A piece of paper with
  three of [ ] + [ ] = [ ],
  one below the other,
  labelled **a**, **b** and **c**.

- For **Lucky Guesses**,
  a sheet with
  two of [ ] + [ ] = [ ] listed
  for each **a**, **b** and **c**.

- Ten cards
  or pieces of paper
  with numerals **0** to **9**.

- Stickers with happy faces.

To play **Lucky Guess** each player gets a game sheet.

Tell the players that the number names for zero to nine are on the ten cards.

Repeat the following requests several times,
- *Name a number that is on the cards.*
- *Name a number that is not on the cards.*

The goal of the game is to guess the names of the numbers that were drawn and to print an equation that is true.

Draw two cards from the deck.
Calculate and announce the sum.

The players make one guess about what numbers they think were drawn that would equal the announced sum.

The players record the guess in the boxes of the equation beside the letter **a**.

Record on a piece of paper or on the chalkboard the statement:
The answer is ___, with the answer shown.

Ask the players to suggest all of the true addition equations that they can think of for the answer.

As the players suggest equations, record these under:
The answer is ___.

Repeat this recording until there are no more responses to,
- *Who can think of an equation that is true which looks
  in any way different from those that have been recorded?*
  5 + 3 = [ ] and **3 + 5 = [ ]** are viewed as different.

The two cards drawn are shown.

A player lucky enough to use the two number names in either order to write a true equation receives or draws three happy faces.

A player who records different equations that are true receives or draws two happy faces.

A player who records an equation that is 'close to being true' receives or draws one happy face, but the player is asked to explain how to change the equation to make it true.

(continued next page ...)

Prior to each new round of guesses, ask a player to explain two different ways, other than counting, and to show that the answer is correct.

After three or more rounds of guesses, the happy faces are counted to find out who is *happiest* or *luckiest* and who is almost as *happy* or *lucky*.

The second version of the game sheet, or *Lucky Guesses,* requires a player to record two different guesses for each announced sum. The procedure is the same as for **Lucky Guess**.

The scoring for this sheet can be changed to:
- four happy faces for recording the two number names as part of the first equation.
- three happy faces for recording the two number names as part of the second equation.
- two happy faces if different pairs of number names were used to record true equations.
- one happy face if a player is able to explain how an equation that is not true can be changed into one that is true.

Rather than drawing the cards at random, select two that are, for one reason or another, deemed appropriate for the players at that time.

To make doubles like **6 + 6 = [ ]** part of the game setting, use a deck of cards with two of each of the numerals **1** to **9**.

Lucky Cover-Up

Materials:

- Two cardboard strips each marked off into ten squares showing the numerals from **1** to **10**, respectively.

  The size of the squares allows for the placement of chips, bottle caps or buttons.

- Two number cubes with **1** to **6** on the faces.

- Chips, buttons or bottle caps.

The game is for two players or two teams.

The goal of **Lucky Cover-Up** is to cover more numerals than the opponent and that the sum of the numerals left uncovered is less than that of the opponent.

Roll the number cubes.

Let us assume a **6** and a **5** are showing.

Calculate the answer, **6 + 5 = 11**, and cover the answer on the game board in whatever way possible and in whatever way deemed most advantageous in terms of the goals of the game.

Some possibilities for covering 11 include:

    10 and 1   9 and 2   8 and 3   5, 4 and 2   6, 4 and 1

Looking at the game board and examining it for possible combinations for a given sum presents several opportunities for the strategy of *guess and test*. As this strategy is employed, true equations as well as equations that are not true will be processed.

Ideally, the goal is to cover all number names, but since that may not happen very often, the sum of the number names left uncovered is the player's score for the game.

When two children play against each other, they can take turns rolling the number cubes and watch each other making the moves or, one child proceeds and goes as far as possible before the other child gets a turn.

The game may also be played without an opponent. A child playing this game alone sets out to try to cover all number names, or to get a sum that is less than the one for the previous try or tries.

While playing the game ask children to talk about all of the possible combinations they can come up with for a sum and tell why certain number names are covered, while others are not. Older children may use the game to discover and describe strategies for the moves they make and the strategies they think are favourable as far as the goal of the game is concerned.

Record Sheet Suggestions

       The observations are of a general nature because there are no specific goals for problem solving and games. Nevertheless, these observations are important. It is more valuable for children to be *curious thinkers* who use their *imaginations* and *love to learn,* than for them to memorize numerous isolated skills. Insight about these desirable characteristics is gained in problem solving and game playing settings.

       We sincerely hope children will encounter many teachers along the way who emphasize *willingness to take risks, eagerness to ask questions* and *high self-esteem* rather than focusing on how much children memorize or how quickly they can respond to given prompts.

1. Indicators of *willingness to talk.* _____

_____

2. Indicators of *willingness to try* things and to make up things. _____

_____

3. Indicators of *thinking* or *thinking about thinking.* _____

_____

4. Indicators of *flexible thinking.* _____

_____

5. Indicators of *curiosity.* _____

_____

6. Indicators of *spontaneity.* _____

_____

7. Indicators of *connecting.* _____

_____

8. Signs of using *imagination.* _____

_____

9. Indicators of *high self-esteem.* _____

_____

ISBN 142518418-9

9 781425 184186